Money isn't God

To my wife Lorrie
who stayed with me
on my pilgrimage
from disenchantment to
determination.

MONEY ISN'T GOD

So why is the church worshipping it?

John White

Inter-Varsity Press

INTER-VARSITY PRESS
38 De Montfort Street, Leicester LE1 7GP, England

Revised edition: © 1993 by John White.
First edition: © 1977 by Inter-Varsity Christian Fellowship
of the United States of America. Published under the title
The Golden Cow.

Unless otherwise stated, Scripture quotations in this
publication are from the Holy Bible, New International
Version. Copyright © 1973, 1978, 1984 International Bible
Society. Published in Great Britain by Hodder & Stoughton
Ltd.

Revised edition published in Great Britain in 1993 by
arrangement with InterVarsity Press, USA.

British Library Cataloguing in Publication Data
A catalogue record for this book is available from the British
Library.

ISBN 0–85110–872–5

Set in Linotron Baskerville
Photoset by Parker Typesetting Service, Leicester
Printed in Great Britain by
Cox & Wyman Ltd, Reading, Berkshire

*Inter-Varsity Press is the book-publishing division of the Universities
and Colleges Christian Fellowship (formerly the Inter-Varsity
Fellowship), a student movement linking Christian Unions in
universities and colleges throughout the United Kingdom and the
Republic of Ireland, and a member movement of the International
Fellowship of Evangelical Students. For information about local and
national activities write to UCCF, 38 De Montfort Street, Leicester
LE1 7GP.*

Contents

Preface

Why a new edition for this book?

The immediate reason is that there is a demand for one. When *The Golden Cow* went out of print I shrugged my shoulders and said, 'Too bad! Guess it's shot its bolt,' and proceeded with other things. But slowly booksellers began to request its reappearance, and in time the folks at Inter-Varsity Press, USA, began to wonder whether a reprint, at least, might be in order.

How the situation in the western church has changed in the years since I wrote the book! Yet the materialism with which the book charged both the West and the western church has not changed; in fact, we have moved further down that road. If *The Golden Cow* was in any sense prophetic, then it received the standard treatment for prophetic utterance – it was largely ignored. Not entirely. It made its small impact. Still, it was powerless to stop the western church's headlong pursuit of material wealth and acceptance of the world's values.

The judgments it and similar books predicted have begun to come to pass, as well as others we did not predict. The Gulf War has come and gone, leaving an uneasy peace in its wake. Communism has been weighed in God's balances and found wanting. The Berlin Wall is no more. Doctrinaire communism is crumbling and, though by no means dead, is so radically wounded that its end is foreseen by many. Judgment has also begun to fall on western Christian leaders of public prominence. Sins have been exposed. A television ministry is no more, and other ministries seem threatened. Many churches have ceased to exist, and other new ones have come into existence. The international situation now seems more volatile than it has been for a long time.

However, if there was any validity in *The Golden Cow*'s prophetic note, then my duty is to do what prophets have always been supposed to do: to continue to cry whether or not people heed. If judgment looms larger (and that is my profound conviction), then I must continue to warn of wrath to come.

I know more about divine judgment now than when I wrote *The Golden Cow*. The topic has haunted me during the intervening years. I am horrified by its awesome nature, so that in *Money Isn't God* I talk about it much more. I know more about idolatry, have experienced the great ferocity of the powers of darkness. They and all the powers of hell are soon to be unleashed by a sovereign God to vent their fury on us. For long years he has been restraining them. They are his pawns of judgment, and judgment is now at the door.

I cry out, not only because it is my duty but because I am impelled to by an inner urgency I cannot resist. But there is more. Gloom and doom form only one side of the picture. The deeper the darkness, the brighter and more powerful shines the light. No darkness can exist where light starts shining. Just as Isaiah predicted, 'the people walking in darkness have seen a great light; on those living in the land of the shadow of death a light has dawned' (Is. 9:2). It is the same today. Matthew 4:16 gives us only the glorious beginning of the fulfilment of Isaiah's prophecy. True prophecy, arising as it does in divine truth, must echo itself in ever-growing volume, and we are now hearing those resounding echoes.

The urgency that impels me is partly that of a warning cry, but much more it is a great trumpet blast of joy. I see triumph ahead, triumph for a revived church and a humbled and repentant Israel. All over the world the signs of revival can no longer be ignored. It is this that must precede Christ's return – not the triumph of darkness that J. N. Darby and, earlier, Edward Irving predicted.

I am delighted to send out this revised and expanded book, to let it join the chorus of many voices that cry both terrible warnings and, at the same time, the amazing goodness and mercy of God. For he *will* triumph. His foes *will* be vanquished, his enemies scattered.

And the time draws near.

It is customary to let the adversities and ardours

of editors go unsung. The manuscript I originally wrote raised one or two vexatious technical problems, and I was so impressed by the professional skill, the diplomacy and the patience of Mr Andrew Le Peau and Dr James Sire that I do not hesitate to break with custom and express my gratitude to them.

Part one:
The allurements
of Lord Mammon

Chapter One

The root of evil

Money. The love of money. If any sin seems to dominate our society, it is the pursuit of material things – that is, making them so important that they take the place of God. True, we have many other sins. And one sin opens the way for another. But if there is a key to the whole business in the West it is materialism.

In recent years, some Muslims have used the phrase 'the Great Satan' to express their feelings about the West and specifically about the United States. Philip Yancey points out that when Muslims think of us, they are thinking of our materialism.

> When the word describes the pursuit of wealth and consumer comforts, few Arab nations disapprove: thanks to oil revenues, the Persian Gulf is the wealthiest region in

the world. But materialism also refers to a philosophical approach, a belief that human life consists mainly (or solely) in what takes place here and now, in the world of matter.

The disciples of Islam tend to view us as being obsessively concerned with this life, not with eternity to come. . . .[1]

Once God ceases to be God in our lives, eternity fades in importance even in Christian thinking. We become materialists both philosophically and behaviourally. At that point the pseudo-deity Lord Mammon takes over our thinking and controls our wills. The philosophical deception is Satanic; our actions come to reflect Lord Mammon, whom we covertly worship.

We all have seen this type of covert worship revealed in the church. A few years ago we were dismayed at two TV evangelists who created scandals because of sexual sin. One was jailed for deception and misappropriation of funds. Though the other case was not as extreme, I suspect that materialism contributed to it also. Are private jet planes necessary to those who proclaim the gospel? What happens to western government officials who abuse travel by government planes?

Am I right in saying that materialism is our predominant sin? Even though no Christian would say money is God, I believe we are guilty of worshipping it. At any rate, that is the issue this book will examine, for it seems to be the chief reason among many that we may soon hear the hoofbeats of the four horses of the Apocalypse. I believe that materialism is about to bring the judgment of God in a horrendous form on the West. Our days may nearly be numbered.

God's judgment

God's judgment? On us? On the West? On his people? Is it possible? The mind reels at such questions. The heart quakes. Judgment is a theme I shall take up at greater length in later chapters. Here let me give a few preliminary thoughts.

Recently I watched heart-rending pictures on television. Bangladesh reported hundreds of thousands dead and ten million people homeless after monsoon flooding. The homeless needed water, supplies, shelter – and the monsoon season was just starting with cholera breaking out among them.

Following news of the Bangladesh tragedy were shots of Peruvians with cholera and a map revealing the spread of the epidemic into Ecuador, Chile, Bolivia and Brazil. Medical supplies were grossly inadequate and water was polluted. A massive, continent-wide plague threatened.

The same day a report from the Horn of Africa made it clear that at least twenty million people faced imminent starvation – between thirteen and fifteen million in Sudan and Ethiopia alone. One report stated that the situation was potentially far worse than the 1984 famine there, another, that it was already worse. Aid was totally inadequate and pessimism prevailed.

By the time you read this, the whole business will be over. Shocking and numbing news will have ceased to shock and numb. But I have the feeling as I sit and type that we are just starting.

Shared judgment

In the Bible, such events were consistently seen as judgments poured out by God. We shrink from thinking of starving Africans as coming under God's judgment (even though there is nothing inconsistent about showing mercy to those God judges). We think of them as 'poor, innocent victims' and regard any suggestion to the contrary as arrogant and judgmental. We say they are the victims of the exploitation and indifference of rich nations, or of the cruelty of vicious tyrants whose only interest is personal glory and power.

True. What we fail to see is that every nation on earth faces judgment because all of humanity sins. God brings judgment on us partly by sending awesome catastrophes and partly by using one another's sin, the sin in our case being economic exploitation.

One day people came to Jesus, musing over God's judgment on people who were victims of a cruel act by Pilate. Jesus did not rebuke them for judgmentalism, but warned that they were in the same boat. 'Do you think that these Galileans were worse sinners than all the other Galileans because they suffered this way? I tell you, no! But unless you repent, you too will all perish' (Lk. 13:2–3).

The clouds *are* gathering. Storms begin to rage about us, perhaps more than they have ever raged in history. Divine judgments on the church and on the world lash whiplike on our shoulders. Why the lash of whips? What has happened to us? Have we sinned in some special way? Is what is

16

happening around us described in the Bible?

Let me begin with God's judgments. God is seen in both Old and New Testaments as the rightful Ruler of the universe. As Creator and Ruler he executes judgment. Since his power is limitless, he can and does send wars, horrendous plagues, tempests and earthquakes to discipline rebellious human beings. Sometimes he exterminates vast numbers of us, as he did at the time of the flood. He made us and has the right to dispose of us. He visits judgment on individuals, cities and nations.

In the Old Testament God commanded Israel to exterminate whole nations (Dt. 7:1–5). He deliberately used heathen kings to punish his own people by conquering and enslaving them. The Bible describes the greatest period of judgment by catastrophes and wars at the close of human history, a period many Christians feel is just round the corner.

The church is not exempt. In the New Testament we watch God's judgment in action – against Ananias and Sapphira, against members of the church in Corinth, and threatened against five of the Asian churches in Revelation. Is it not a little naive to suppose that nothing similar will happen to us? To us in the West? To us in the western church?

At the same time, the Bible describes God as patient and merciful. Even his most terrible judgments have a holy purpose. For generations, warning and pleading, he has consistently waited a long time before acting. Though his eventual actions are horrendously severe, he aims to purge hopeless situations and to bring repentance where he can. And if his people heed neither prophetic

17

warnings nor the initial stages of judgment, then he makes sure a godly remnant survives. John tells us that God's essential nature is love (1 Jn. 4:8). It is this side of his nature that we are more familiar with; we forget that love can breed jealousy.

Principles of judgment

Few Christians seem to understand that the tragedies, wars and catastrophic judgments represent only the end point of a long process which evolves over centuries. Judgment proceeds in determined stages which we will look at more closely in a later chapter. The first stage consists of spiritual blindness in the person or nation being judged and is followed by several more phases, each arising out of the preceding phase. Only when we still refuse to turn, after seeing the stupidity of our rebellion, does he unsheathe his naked sword.

Principle: *Catastrophe is an end point, preceded by warnings and by a painful reaping of the consequences of our wrong actions.*

Judgment in the form of catastrophe follows persistent sin. Our sins, both within the church and in society, are of every variety. Yet while all sins flourish everywhere, some places are known for a special brand of sin – San Francisco for homosexuality, for example. Some Bible students feel that an ancient god or spirit may rule over an area where a particular sin predominates. I am not aware of any Bible passage which makes this explicit, though it is consistent with certain other passages dealing with such spirits. There are governing spirits, some of greater authority and

18

power than others. They seem to be fallen angelic beings, ruling under the general suzerainty of Satan, 'the god of this world'.

Daniel's prayer was not answered for three weeks because an angelic messenger was held up by the prince (or king) of Persia (possibly a reference to an evil spirit; see Dn. 10:1–13). Certainly, too, as we shall see later, Christians can come under bondage to such beings, and this can be part of God's judgment. However, we cannot blame angelic evil beings for our condition. They can only rule us when we nibble the delicacies they offer.

Principle: *When as individuals we pursue a particular sin, we are in danger of returning to bondage by dark powers, the bondage Christ delivered us from; when a society does so, the same rule holds*.

When the earth opened up

When the horror of our blinded, sin-controlled condition fails to cause us to cry out in distress to God, catastrophic forms of judgment follows. In Old Testament times God executed the final stages of his judgment by sending plague, natural catastrophes, war, captivity and death. He took no delight in doing so, showing himself to be patient, long-suffering, plenteous in mercy. The horrific nature of the judgments reflected the gravity of sin. Always God's aim was to purge and to purify the people through whom he planned to carry out his saving purposes.

Let us look at one of these acts of judgment. We must examine at close range the details, even though they seem horrendous. They are described in the Bible for a good reason. Take the

19

incident of Korah's rebellion in Numbers 16. Backed by a dissatisfied group of leading Levites, Korah, himself a Levite, along with a couple of non-Levites, Dathan and Abiram, protested against the leadership of Aaron and Moses (Nu. 16:1–10). They aimed at supplanting the Aaronic priestly succession.

You will never understand the incident unless you grasp that the nation was at that time led not by Moses, still less by Aaron, but by God. He led the people supernaturally, by the pillar of fire and cloud. More importantly he shared his heart with Moses 'face to face', communicating his truth, his wishes, his instructions through Moses. God told Moses what to say, and Moses instructed the people. Mostly it worked well. The people were impressed by the evidences of Moses' intimacy with God, by the sign of the pillar of cloud and fire, and by Yahweh's deliverances. However, there were also times when the system seemed to fail. The people's eyes would be more on themselves than on God. Discontent would arise.

People find it easier to grumble against leadership than against God. In this case the rebellion, apparently against Moses and Aaron, is in fact rebellion against God. Probably manipulated by the king-makers Dathan and Abiram, Korah insisted on being chief negotiator with God, replacing the powerful duo of Moses and Aaron.

I will not dwell on the details in the earlier part of the story, but pick it up at the point where judgment falls. Dathan and Abiram had defiantly stayed in their tents, refusing to speak to Moses.

Moses, instructed by God, warned the Israelites to stand clear of the area around the tents. 'As soon as he finished saying all this, the ground under them split apart, and the earth opened its mouth and swallowed them, with their households and all Korah's men and all their possessions. They went down alive into the grave, with everything they owned; the earth closed over them, and they perished and were gone from the community. At their cries, all the Israelites around them fled' (Nu. 16:31–34).

Can you imagine it? The sudden appalling awareness of imminent and horrendous death. Brief glimpses of the terrified faces of family members. Men, women, children falling with shrieks into the great jaw of the earth, along with their tents, their animals, their household goods. Did the earth's mouth close shut with a roar? Certainly there was noisy panic. 'At their cries, all the people around them fled, shouting, "The earth is going to swallow us too!"' Hours later did a cloud of dust hang over an area from which homes and living flesh had vanished with dreadful suddenness?

The tragedy was that the process of catastrophic judgment had only begun. At the same time judgment fell on the waiting Levites, standing before God with their censers: 'And fire came out from the LORD and consumed the 250 men who were offering the incense' (Nu. 16:35).

Then calamity followed calamity. The people had grasped neither the significance nor the seriousness of what had happened. They presumed that the tragedy represented a display of wizardry by Moses rather than divine displeasure.

So they rose up against Moses, and by a further stroke of God's judgment nearly fifteen thousand people lost their lives. Only the desperate intercession of Moses and Aaron stayed God's hand.

It may seem to be a fearful and foolhardy defiance of a holy God for Moses and Aaron to run, censers in their hands, to plead the cessation of the plague. Yet it is what God wants us to do now. For while many will be granted repentance, some will not escape. Let us plead for the spirit of repentance to be poured out!

In spite of the reality of approaching judgment, I am filled with joyful expectation. Repentance and revival are coming. Let us repent in so far as we are able. Let us cry to God to visit his people, that the revelation of his real purposes may give him glory.

The severity of God's judgments

Can this really be our God – the God who opens the earth to swallow his own followers? The God who consumes grumblers with fire?

In Old Testament and New, the picture is the same. Is God a cruel tyrant? Why are the judgments so severe? The example we have glanced at is but one of many, others being more horrendous yet. They begin with the flood and continue with God's instructions to Joshua about the 'devoted' nations occupying Canaan (Jos. 6 – 7). Do you remember God's judgment upon Israel following David's conceited head-count of his people? Even on God's own people terrible judgment fell, as they went as slaves to foreign lands, most of them never to return, and the northern kingdom disappeared from the face of the earth.

I will not attempt to explain his severity. This

God is *my* God and I am his creature, not his judge. Our difficulty with it arises from two factors.

First we lack an awareness of who and what God is. He is a God of burning holiness as well as a God of compassion. He cannot stand sin.

Second, our horror would diminish if we could grasp how evil sin is. We are so used to sin. (Human beings can get used to almost anything. Fresh air smells scary when you have breathed foulness all your life.)

Years ago in Bolivia my one-year-old first-born son fell and split the skin and flesh beneath his chin, exposing the floor of his mouth. We were in the wilds, miles from the nearest hospital, and I lacked surgical equipment. Friends crowded around and held him – arms, hands, feet, legs, head – while I trimmed the wound with inadequate scissors. Then with eyebrow tweezers and a darning needle I sewed skin and tissues together. We had no anaesthetic. I will never forget my little son's screams of terror and pain or my own agony in having to inflict it. How I wished I could explain to him why I was doing what I was doing.

That experience gives me some notion of how God feels when he acts in judgment. God is profoundly moved by his people's sufferings, even when those sufferings are a response to their own wickedness:

> In all their distress he too was distressed,
>   and the angel of his presence saved them.
> In his love and mercy he redeemed them;
>   he lifted them up and carried them
>   all the days of old.

(Is. 63:9)

God never loses his love for sinners. Quoting Hosea, Jesus once said, '"I desire mercy, not sacrifice." For I have not come to call the righteous, but sinners' (Mt. 9:13). But let us remember one thing – he will not hold back for ever. And as for the West with our worship of money, let us not forget that the judgment millennia ago on worshippers of the golden calf was bloody and terrifying. Yet still a grieving God tells us: 'For I desire mercy, not sacrifice, and acknowledgment of God rather than burnt offerings' (Ho. 6:6).

My little son had no idea what could have happened had infection developed in the floor of his mouth. He only knew the terror of a cruel father inflicting unbelievable pain on him. Our problem with God is no different.

The urgency of our situation

This book is an updated, revised and reorganized version of a book I wrote over a dozen years ago, *The Golden Cow*. Its message is just as urgent now as it was when first published, and perhaps more so. To emphasize this I have added three new chapters (this chapter, chapter thirteen and chapter fifteen) which especially examine the postulate that God's coming judgment on the West has been earned in part – perhaps even in large measure – by our materialism. Since the church in the West is guilty of the same sin, judgment is already coming upon her too. Most of the chapters that follow examine what materialism is, in what ways we are guilty of it and why it is so important.

The rest of part one presents a case for how our local churches, parachurch organizations and Christian businesses have subjected themselves to

24

mammon rather than to Christ. Chapter two considers the power that property plays, especially in local congregations. In chapter three we look at the pitfalls of paying pastors according to a double standard. The next chapter examines the fund-raising techniques that often accompany Christian ministries. The pressure to compete and grow in Christian organizations is the topic of chapter five. Then in the following chapter we review the booming business of selling what has become known as 'Jesus junk' and 'holy hardware'. The subject covered in the last chapter of this section is how a materialistic mind-set has affected the way we approach people in evangelism – do we treat them as objects we win or as people we kneel with before God's throne?

Part two is concerned with how Jesus and the prophets reacted when God's people followed other gods. Chapter eight deals with Christ's own enactment of prophetic wrath and displeasure with religious leaders. In chapters nine and ten I define my terms. Why did the prophets use the image of prostitution to symbolize the guilt of God's people? Chapter eleven looks carefully at the issue of our possessions. Then in chapter twelve I try to provide an overview of those ways in which the church has attached herself to mammon, rather than to her true bridegroom, Christ.

In the last section of the book, I begin in chapter thirteen by returning to the question with which we started, looking more carefully at the way God's judgment begins and develops. Chapters fourteen and fifteen conclude by considering how God wants us to respond in light of all that has been said. Judgment is not the only option. I examine the nature of repentance, what it is, how it takes place and what its results are.

For, as I stated earlier in this chapter, God takes no pleasure in judgment. Rather, he is the God who weeps over our sins and grieves over our waywardness. He yearns for us to realize there is no place for two treasures in our hearts. He seeks to win back his bride from her false lover.

Chapter Two

The power of property

Some years ago when I applied for membership in an evangelical church, one of its leaders mentioned to me the importance the privileges of membership would give me. He stressed the necessity that my application and my doctrinal beliefs be properly screened. Because I thought of membership in terms of fellowship, of discipline and of prayer I promptly concurred. My friend (a warm Christian) cut me short.

'Your words would carry a lot of weight, and there are hundreds of thousands of dollars tied up in this property,' he told me. 'The way you vote could influence the way many other people vote.'

I was astounded and begged him to clarify his statement. But as he went on talking, there could be no doubt about it. At that point he was viewing me not just as a brother in Christ but as a potential financial power in the church.

I do not believe that my friend's attitude (shocking as it may seem to some people) was anything extraordinary. For the basic issue when you reach rock bottom in many church quarrels is who gets control of the real estate.

If we were to worship the gods of materialism in the secrecy of our hearts or even of our households, the matter would be bad enough. But it is inevitable that, blinded as we are to our error, we have moulded our churches by the values that govern our own lives. In this chapter I shall consider a key indicator of our spiritual condition – our concern for property.

In so doing we shall be able to answer a number of pressing questions. Do we in the church worship money? If so, how is it seen? For what is the church deserving of judgment? Are we blind to what the whole world sees?

The stones cry out

The truth is that we preach and we parade to ourselves. While we proclaim that eternity matters more than time and the spirit more than body, while we urge one another to give to the work of our Lord, while we render tithes and offerings, the world ignores our pious performances. The stones of our lovely buildings cry out to passers-by while the voices from our pulpits remain muffled and dead. The stones boast, 'We are the symbols of Christ today. Look at us if you want to know what Christians care about.'

They tell the truth. We care very much about them. It seems we argue more heatedly about property than we ever do about doctrine. In fact, sometimes when we appear to be arguing about

28

doctrine we are actually arguing about control of lands, funds and buildings.

Christian groups of all kinds are far too *thing*-centred. It is very easy to raise money for a project when the project has something tangible (like a clinic building, a school or a mobile gospel unit with a portable movie screen to show gospel films in villages, and so on), especially if the project has a sentimental or a romantic appeal. People give to something that looks good in a picture. But to find the money to pay a pastor a reasonable wage is all too difficult.

Because Christian organizations are property-centred, their programmes become property-bound. Once you have bought an expensive building (or boat or plane), you have to justify its existence. The argument that prevails when plans are made runs like this: 'Well, it seems to me, brother, that we've got a wonderful plane costing thousands of dollars, and we're only using it once a month. ...' So a missionary operation, for example, begins to centre on planes, boats, buildings.

Planes, boats and buildings are all of value, but too often (without our realizing it) they master us rather than serve us. They sit on our boards and committees and cast their silent votes on every motion.

People tell me it is impossible to go without things. 'How could we run our missionary society without buildings and equipment? We would be crippled without them.' Exactly. Because the programme has become geared to things, it cannot possibly survive without things. And because western Christian mentality tends to think in terms of things, it can conceive no other way to operate.

Nor is this all. We like to think that our evangelistic and church-building endeavours are planned prayerfully with ultimate goals in view. Not so. They are governed more by the mass psychology of church members than by prayerful planning. Why do I say this? I say it because ordinary church members respond to what they can understand. And they understand things. If you can link in their minds the conversions of Indians with a plane or if you can persuade them of the value that owning a hotel will have for training evangelists, you will open their wallets.

And the bigger the operation the better. Be they rich or poor, the effect on them will be the same. As they realize that their few pounds will provide a springboard for a massive evangelistic assault, they grow intoxicated with wonder. Money from people all around them pours into Operation Big Deal.

The phrases *God has supplied* and *God has opened the way* are pious phrases that too often mean, 'There's more money available for this sort of project, so that's what we'd better do.' Consequently, the projects that bloom, or at least that create the illusion of blooming, are determined by what most appeals to those who have the least experience in Christian work as money is given in response to the manipulation of Christian entrepreneurs. In the days of Joe McCarthy any Christian radio programme knocking communism was on to a good thing.

The consequences on Christian work itself are not quite so serious as it might at first appear; the real evil lies in our attitude.

In the long run

Church-building committees work on a principle which has much to commend it: spending a little more money initially will save later. For example, a panelled wall will never need painting and 'will always look good'. If anyone criticizes the expenditure on the ground that churches should be helping the poor or the missionaries and be less concerned with the building, the reply runs, 'Yes, but we'll actually be *saving* money. If we have to help the poor or the mission field, *in the long run* we'll be able to give them more.'

'In the long run.' When will that be? What happens to the needy in the meantime? And do we seriously suppose that the best way to help the poor is for us to use expensive building materials?

Other pseudo-profundities cause us all to nod heads in solemn agreement. 'It really represents a saving.' 'Nothing is too good for God.' 'People are attracted to nice buildings.' (What sort of people? Down-and-outs? People on social security? Winos? Whom do we *wish* to attract?) 'We mustn't give the impression that the Christian message is cheap.' And so on and so on.

Jesus was accused of eating with publicans and sinners. More than one immoral woman felt at ease in his presence. The poor thronged around him. He had come, he said, to preach the gospel to them.

But we, his modern followers, have sealed ourselves in middle-class religious ghettos. By our dress, our hair styles, our church buildings, we have raised impenetrable psychological barriers around us, effectively shutting out many who need our Redeemer.

Yet if I leave the impression that there is something wrong with good church buildings, I have failed to make my point clear. It is not *possessing* riches that God condemns, but clinging to them, coveting them and centring our activity around them. It is our wrong way of looking at things, our wrong scale of values, that matters. It is not meeting in a good building that is wrong, but making such a building a priority and fooling ourselves into believing that we can't get on without it. It is building with unnecessary luxury at a time when inequity abounds, thinking more of the building than of the church, more of a good organ than of praise, more of the communion table than of the body and blood of Christ.

'Ah, I'm so glad he got round to making this important distinction,' someone whispers. 'That means we needn't feel guilty about our very fine property and such a *functional* building.'

But hold on. There are quite a few churches like yours in lower-middle-class and middle-class sectors in your city. What is going on among the poor? Among the recent immigrants? Among the motley international groups of newcomers struggling to gain a foothold on the lower end of the economic ladder? Do we relegate them all to the ministries of the nineteenth-century city missions? Or do we take some responsibility ourselves?

How necessary are the costly facilities of the 'functional' structures we have created? How important is it that our young people play volleyball in an 'adequate gymnasium'? How necessary is that beautiful Christian education wing? Who from the congregation would be willing to play volleyball with immigrants on a piece of waste ground? Or begin Sunday-school classes in the dreary tenements that surround it? I understand a certain reluctance lest 'our young people' be exposed to that sort of thing. I also understand that the denizens of the inner-city netherworld would feel thoroughly out of place in our luxurious facilities. So what should we do?

I can think of two suggestions. The first would be for the leadership of the church to meet and prayerfully consider the church's responsibilities to neglected areas such as those I have mentioned. Surely God could place a burden on someone's heart for them. Could there not be a prayerful laying of hands on some who are called to minister elsewhere? To research specific areas and talk to those who know about them? To raise autonomous home fellowships?

My second suggestion is to the expanding church, the church that plans to build 'a more adequate facility'. My advice is don't. The constant argument is that 'it's always cheaper in the long run to own your own' plane or house, rather than to rent it. Owning your own transportation gets you somewhere faster and more conveniently. I remember a young missionary who urged a middle-aged veteran jungle evangelist to go to a faraway village by plane rather than by Indian dugout. 'You could be there in an hour,' he pleaded. 'The way you are going you'll take days – four days cooped up in a canoe with five Indians. Think of all the time you could save.'

Churches should rethink priorities. Can city-centre facilities be rented for public meetings? Can home study groups become heavenly leaven, changing the nature of the core area? Can

33

imaginative schemes be thought up to attract the youth of the area? If so, let your congregation divide. Let those who feel comfortable in your present facility stay there. Let the rest move out to reach the downtrodden.

I must warn you of course to beware of naivety as much as of condescension. But you won't remain naive long. And real love and respect for people leave no room for condescension.

As for our private wealth and our lovely homes, there are many things we can do. We can see that the 'guest room' has a higher occupancy rate. We can set up a church organization through which a distress-alert system brings us the abandoned wives and other temporarily distressed persons so that they can find their feet and start life anew themselves. We can invite such needy souls not as guests to whom we show gracious hospitality but as full members of the family who share its joys, its sorrows, its prayers, its celebrations and its day-to-day tasks. Our carpets will wear out faster. Our settees will begin to sag sooner. Our favourite records will get scratched. But since when were we called to live for carpets, settees and stereos?

And how about cars? I just made the discovery that it takes me ten minutes longer to get to work by bus than by car. So now we're a one-car family (still in a luxury class to be sure, for one car is way above one bicycle) and that saves us in Canada around $200 monthly. In how many more ways can we free up money for those in need?

I am deliberately sidestepping the question of whether constructing a beautiful building might not itself be an act of worship to God. I do so, not because the question is unimportant, but because it is irrelevant. We do not in fact build beautiful buildings from a spirit of worship but for prestige and pride.

Chapter Three

Paying the pastor

Our corporate materialism is seen not only in our attitude to buildings and facilities of every kind, but also in our attitude to pastors and Christian workers.

Running a club

I meet many pastors. Some I instruct in pastoral counselling, and others I treat as patients. Often as we have talked together the matter of materialism comes up. Some pastors confess they have to battle against a materialistic spirit in themselves, finding that they, too, are influenced by a materialistic culture.

Most of them agree with me that their congregations are too *thing*-centred. Some confess to feelings of resentment as they observe members of the congregation growing rich while they themselves make little or no material advance.

Their problem is not simply one of covetousness but of feeling forsaken. It seems to many of them that members of their congregation are too busy making money to care deeply enough about the spiritual responsibilities of entering into the pastor's struggles. Occasionally a pastor may actually be told, 'That's the sort of thing we pay *you* to do.'

It is unwise to generalize, for certainly many Christians are active in their local churches. But too many pastors get the feeling of being paid to run a kind of Christian club. Sunday-school teachers and others who help with the programme are like volunteer workers who know little of the agony and pain of pastoral burdens. Their main concern is often that the pastor doesn't show enough interest in *them*.

I occasionally come across pastors who look on their salaries as thirty pieces of silver. 'They are giving me money,' they will say, 'so they can excuse themselves from a spiritual burden God would lay on their shoulders. And like a Judas I take it.' While a few pastors luxuriate in high salaries, others battle with resentment over poor wages. To ask for more money after preaching a sermon on self-sacrifice would be impossible. Yet why, the pastor feels, should he or she take the major spiritual burden while receiving inadequate pay so others can be set free to make their piles?

Some pastors, as I mentioned, are generously paid and grateful for it. Others moonlight to make ends meet and feel guilty about doing so. Yet others (for greedy pastors exist, some of them nothing more than religious psychopaths) cheat on expenses, manipulate the mission funds or hint about their needs to rich old ladies.

Many, saddened at heart and burdened with a sense of failure, are leaving the pastorate. They feel frustrated, spiritually empty, lonely and bewildered by a schizophrenic sensation of being looked up to in spiritual matters and looked down on in the area that really counts – that of financial success. For money in our culture is a mark of greatness. If you can grumble about taxes, put a large cheque in the offering and buy a mink coat, then you are someone indeed.

From the pulpit pastors may look down on the materialism of the rich. But making pastoral calls, they eye their brothers' and sisters' beautiful clothes and their own shabby suits and suddenly feel cheap. They tell themselves that treasure in heaven is what matters, but the words no longer bring them comfort.

Partners or employee?

It is easy for people who have not stood where a pastor stands to accuse him or her of 'being defeated'. The question is not *whether* he or she is defeated but *why*. Who are we to demand that one person in our midst be paid to stand in spiritual isolation? With our words and our handshakes we say, 'We're with you all the way.' But by our actions we communicate quite clearly that we have other more important matters to attend to. We are not the pastor's partner. He or she is our paid employee. And we are sometimes proud that we treat our employee so generously.

When every aspect has been considered, what matters most to a good pastor is not the size of the salary but what that money means. If it seems to express loving concern and a desire to share freely, he or she may feel like a millionaire. But if it is payola to keep the pastor tactful towards prominent church members, or if it keeps him or her in the position of the paid hireling of the church board, then the pastor is abjectly poor, however large the pay-cheque may be.

How, in fact, should one decide on a pastor's salary? There is no simple answer. But if you are serious about it, you must address more questions to yourself. Do you need a pastor at all? Some churches don't. If twenty members gave two and a half hours a week to doing what the pastor is paid to do, they would contribute fifty hours a week. Why do we not have the time? Is it because money matters to us? Is it in fact *cheaper* to hire a pastor to do God's work?

I know very well that twenty people giving two and a half hours are not the same as one person giving fifty, but that is beside the point. Churches often hire pastors for the wrong reasons, reasons that are rarely admitted. One is that too few actually *believe* the Holy Spirit can weld the church members into a living, active body. The Holy Spirit can work properly only when you hire a pastor.

Another reason is the one I have already dealt with: we are too busy making money to give the time God would have us give. Do not misunderstand me. I am not arguing against the pastoral office but pointing to its abuses and the ways in which materialism has corrupted the relationship between pastor and flock.

If you are sure you need a pastor, and you have decided the basic principles by which that person should be paid (for example, the number of children he or she has; what the car and housing allowances are worth; what the median income of the church members is), how do you fix the sum? Again, I can only supply you with more questions. If you find yourself getting hung up about money, are you thinking more about money than about the pastor?

What would be wrong with giving your pastor fifty per cent more than whatever sum seems reasonable? Are you afraid it might make him or her too money-conscious? If so, what business did you have appointing this person? If you were in a position to pick a pastor, you should also know that God expects you to discern whether a pastoral candidate has a weakness about money. And if he or she has a weakness about money, you should never have given that person the responsibility of a pastorate (1 Tim. 3:3)!

Some churches like to give high salaries because the pastor's standard of living will affect the kind of people who will attend. (Posh pastor, fancy congregation.) God is concerned with motives, not with amounts. Do you resent the thought of your pastor's having too much money? Then double his or her salary! Why? To show your love. But aren't there better ways of showing love? Of course there are, but why not show your pastor love in these ways too? Do you ask me what happens if the salary is too much for him or her? I answer, that's the pastor's problem. He or she could make the choice to give more money away. Pray that your pastor may have wisdom in handling what he or she doesn't need.

My cynicism makes me realize that the only real difficulty to arise if we doubled all our pastors' salaries would be an increase in the number of would-be pastors. Yet if we were to deal with the deadly disease of our materialism, the problem of having too many pastors around would be a minor one. (Money is a screen to pick out 'spiritual' pastors – double standard.)

Double standards

Throughout the discussion on pastors' salaries I have been avoiding what may be the crux of the matter. We have the unarticulated feeling that people in Christian work *ought* to live more sacrificially than the rest of us. By and large they do. There are wide disparities within each group I shall refer to, and I can only make a rough generalization. But we could say that in order of financial prosperity, ordinary Christians stand at the top of the heap, pastors next, then home mission workers of various sorts, foreign missionaries from the mainline denominations, and finally missionaries from the older (especially European) interdenominational mission groups.

And we are satisfied with the arrangement. This is the way it should be. After all, missionaries are the most spiritual people among us, with pastors next and finally the rest of us just ordinary Christians. It sounds absurd when the words are articulated, but I have talked to too many Christians to be fooled. We feel uncomfortable when it is spelled out, but this is the way we actually see it. In fact, even when I spell it out, some Christians seem surprised that I see anything wrong with the view.

The most glaring error lies in the assumption that God has two standards of living – one for 'full-time' Christians and another for 'part-time', volunteer Christians. For this is what the matter boils down to. The expression *full-time worker* is dangerously misleading, implying that while all of us are Christians all the time, only some of us work for God all the time.

The first danger lies in an artificial separation between the sacred and the secular. For Christians no such separation should exist. Brother Lawrence swept the floor for God. Whatever we do 'in word or deed' must be done for God under his Spirit's direction. It must be done out of love for God and aimed at glorifying him. Christians should be those who wipe their noses, clean their teeth, fold their dirty clothes, write reports, sell merchandise, play the piano and clean the toilet as acts of worship and service to God. It is no more holy to preach an evangelistic sermon than it is to play catch with the children. What makes these actions holy or other-wise is the attitude of heart from which they spring.

But there is a second danger. Once we have accepted the full-time/non-full-time dichotomy we are let off the hook spiritually. It is all very well to talk about being yielded to the Holy Spirit every moment of the day, but we can never be yielded when we accept the idea of a double standard. Say what we like about our dedication. As long as we think of a missionary as being (by virtue of being 'full-time') more dedicated than ourselves, we will automatically set limits on what God demands of us. Only by becoming missionaries can we achieve the ultimate in dedication. Thus (so long as we believe this) we will live less dedicated lives than missionaries. And this is nonsense.

The double standard shows up in our materialism, however. We measure spirituality by doing without. Like any false notion, the idea is a half-truth. Jesus left riches in glory and embraced poverty that we might be made rich. He calls us to forsake all we have to follow him.

Notice two things. First, he calls *all* of us to forsake everything and follow him. Just as there is no division between those who do sacred work and those of us who do secular work, so none exists between groups who are supposed to give up everything to follow him and those who are merely to give tithes and offerings. And for a moment I may set aside the practical difficulty of how we are all supposed to go about giving up all we possess, I must hasten to insist again that we have no right to demand of Christian workers a standard we do not follow ourselves. There is one standard of sacrifice applying equally to every child of God. No-one is exempted from it. Any one of us who claims to be exempt denies the righteous claims of Christ on his or her life.

Second, to give up everything for Christ consists of an *internal* relinquishment of all our possessions. I have covered the matter in an earlier book.[1] The standard set before us is not that all Christians take a vow of poverty. Some of us will always be richer and others poorer. Yet all of us are to have a contract with Christ that whenever obedience to him means sacrifice of any degree, even to losing everything we have or to facing prison and death, then obedience is what matters. The obedience will be all the easier if we daily relinquish to him all we possess.

All Christians are called to be disciples. All

Christians at any time, under any circumstances, are to be ready for new sets of instructions from headquarters which might mean total material loss. So if obedience means that I move to a city where I will make less money or lose my beautiful house, I move, whether I am a missionary or an 'ordinary Christian'.

It is not that riches, nice homes or luxuries of any kind are in themselves bad. They may in fact represent gifts of a loving God, given for our enjoyment. They have their dangers, of course. We get too used to them, too fond of them. Or they can become goals to be achieved. But in themselves they are in no way evil. If our attitude is right we shall inevitably, as I pointed out earlier, share our good homes with those in need of shelter, provided our churches are properly organized to spot and remedy human dilemmas around us quickly and effectively.

Again, the reality of the situation is such that I may in fact be earning more money than a missionary does. There may be no practical way of remedying the discrepancy. But the discrepancy does not necessarily mean that one of us is living a more spiritual life than the other. It is an accident of war, a war we are both equally committed to. Whenever (in spite of very practical difficulties) there is a chance of evening up the discrepancy, all of us ought to be equally eager to do so.

Murder by hair spray

Some writers would at this point rise up to denounce the church in the West for luxuriating in wealth when Christians in other places are starving. And they would be right. We are callous

44

and blind to the world's naked and hungry, be they our Christian brothers and sisters or our fellow human beings. While a devoted Christian woman is bothered because she cannot find her hair spray before setting out for her Sunday-school class, a Sudanese mother is watching her baby's eyes settle into the empty stare of death.

There are two sides to the question, of course. It would be unjust to accuse the Sunday-school teacher of murder by hair spray. There are huge economic and logistical problems about the transfer of wealth and food from rich nations to starving ones. We need not feel condemned because we are surrounded by abundance. Rather, we should praise and thank a bountiful God who pours unmerited blessings upon us.

On the other hand, we have no right to brush the problem aside because of the complications. At the heart of the matter lies our dependence upon material things. We take them for granted. We accumulate them. We go into debt to acquire them, work longer hours to earn them. They enslave us. They enslave not only our bodies but our hearts which no longer have room for the crying of the needy, the starving and the dying.

Here lie the beginnings of our harlotry. We cherish our lovely buildings. We give payola to our pastors and missionaries so they will accept the spiritual responsibility and release us to acquire things. We take our wealth for granted while in our hearts the groans of the starving and the screams of the tortured are muted into background music.

But our guilt does not stop here. We are part of a Christian world into which the worship of money has infiltrated more widely than most of us could ever dream. The church has become unfaithful because her religion has become an industry. It is itself big business. And it is mandatory that we look carefully at the monster we have created. The next chapter continues this investigation by examining the methods of fundraising many Christian organizations have adopted.

Chapter Four

Religious business

Yesterday for the second time in ten minutes I bumped into Mitch on Kennedy Street. 'Oh, Dr White,' he said as we passed, 'the Bible society man said to ask you when his group could get to speak in your church. He said it's the only church in the city they've never spoken in.'

Mitch is rejoicing in his newfound faith in Christ and is unaware at this point of a lot that goes on behind the scenes. I was nettled by the accusation (a false one), less by the Bible society itself (for which I have a profound respect) than by the never-ending pressure on some of us, a pressure that results from competitiveness among Christian institutions.

Why has the pressure arisen? Why do I groan at the pile of Christian junk mail on my desk and shrink from the task of going through it? Have I the right to use words like *Christian junk mail*?

Most organizations tell me that while their own promotional literature is not junk, a great deal of what comes through the mail in Christ's name *is*. But where is the impartial judge of junk? What is it about the system that forces Christian advertisers who fully recognize my negative reaction to the pile of envelopes on my desk, to calculate how they can catch my eye and hold my attention by their particular productions? Why am I a target of so many advertising arrows, ducking and dodging from the archers who shoot them at me? And how can I tell which archers ought to be allowed to wound me most?

The faith principle

There is no simple answer to any of my questions. Nor, as I have already made it plain, is my aim to do a sociological treatise on evangelical fund-raising. Rather, it is to point once more to our reverence of money, which in part at least is behind the pressure. We trust in mass advertising more than we trust in God. We corrode the term *prayer support* to mean 'financial support'. And while we say we are trusting God to work *through* the means we are using to 'acquaint the Christian public', we would feel rather frightened if the means were taken away. Poor old God would be left to stumble along without his crutches.

What we must do is to ask ourselves what we mean by faith in God. Do we really believe in the God of Moses, of Elijah and of Paul? And in asking the questions we need not lose ourselves in theological debate. We can look at the development of the 'faith principle' in the modern missionary movement, its slow corruption and its eventual takeover by business philosophies and techniques within many Christian movements.

In the nineteenth century, people like Hudson Taylor and George Müller grappled with some of the questions I have been raising and pioneered what is now referred to as the faith principle. Taylor took issue with a broad range of practices. He favoured direction of missionary activity from the mission field itself rather than from the home base, since local problems were less readily appreciated at home. And in a day when mission board members included distinguished clergy and members of the aristocracy, Taylor's board members were selected on the basis of their spiritual maturity rather than for their worldly prestige.

But his most exciting departure from the practice of his day had to do with raising funds. Boldly he enunciated the principle of 'moving men's hearts through prayer to God alone' – 'that is to say, without appealing to people directly. God's work done in God's way, he asserted, would never lack God's supplies. Appeals for money were forbidden. Taylor refused to compete financially with other groups. Collections were not taken up at missionary meetings. Following one particular meeting, a large sum of money from a private donor was politely refused. (The donor returned in the morning, saying that God had exercised his heart to give a much larger sum, which was accepted.)

The daring nature of the approach appealed to many people tired of Christian fund-raising. True stories of dramatic instances of God's intervention awoke in the hearts of many Christians a hunger to deal more realistically with the living God. Steadily the method gained credence. As the China Inland Mission (founded by Taylor and now existing as the Overseas Missionary Fellowship) grew in size and prestige, a widening sector of evangelicals began to favour the same faith principle as a *modus operandi* for financing Christian work.

In retrospect, it seems inevitable that the principle grew to be not only widely accepted but also adulterated and coated with hypocrisy. The words *by faith* eventually acquired a technical meaning and constituted a badge of spiritual respectability. Today we scarcely smile at the inconsistency of a Christian television programme's closing with the words, 'As you know, this is a venture of faith. We are looking to God alone to meet *all* our needs, as you his people give generously to support this effort which reaches millions of needy people with the gospel. Our programme costs $250,000 weekly. Please write and encourage us. Your letters mean much. . . . We would like to send you at no charge a booklet entitled . . .' – and so on.

The inconsistency I refer to has nothing to do with asking for money. God's people need not be ashamed to request one another's financial help. The inconsistency lies in the use of the words *by faith in God alone* when an overt advertising stratagem is being used.

In their day, people like Taylor and Müller were doing something more important than enunciating a financial policy. They were re-evaluating their relationship with God. The question with which they grappled had to do with

50

whether they were trusting in people, in methods or in God. It seemed to them that the only way they could be sure they were trusting in God alone was to cut themselves off from what they would otherwise trust in. By all appearances God met them more than halfway. More important than the financial success of the policy was the joy they experienced in a new walk of faith.

Three methods and a fourth

Amy Carmichael once pointed out that Scripture supports three methods of raising funds: asking God's people for money, tentmaking (that is, earning your living to support your Christian service) and trusting God to supply by some means known in advance only to him. A fourth method is not scriptural: to profess to walk by faith in God alone and simultaneously to hint for funds or manipulate people into giving.

The three methods backed by Scripture are not mutually exclusive (Paul used all three), nor is any one method essentially superior to any other. We do not worship methods; we worship God. Therefore, nothing is sacrosanct about the faith principle. I imagine all of us would agree that whatever method we use, our faith should be in God rather than in the method. What distinguishes Hudson Taylor from the rest of us is that he was prepared to risk not only his own material security but also that of a growing body of missionaries to a policy that was insanity – if God was not behind it. I gravely question whether most of us have his kind of courage or faith, whatever we may profess about trusting God. At heart we have more confidence in money.

I receive more pleas than I know what to do with. I cannot possibly read, let alone 'prayerfully consider', the mass of photocopied letters, cards, announcements, photographs and magazines with which the postman staggers to my door.

A lonely widow bereft of friends may find comfort in this mountain of paper. For the 'mite' she lovingly sends from her meagre resources she may receive a heart-warming 'personal letter' (little guessing it to be the synthetic product of a word processor) and even more prayer letters and magazines. Each day she goes eagerly to the letterbox feeling needed. She has become part of a whole much greater than herself. The ache of her loneliness is lessened, and for her the price is worth it. Soon she may offer her savings to the institution in an annuity. It would pay her an 'income' in the form of interest on her death loan, but this interest is often less than what the institution would have to pay on a bank loan.

Do not misunderstand me. It is not the widow who is the loser but the organization. God loves a cheerful giver, so that a widow's mite dropped in the coffers of the modern Sadducees does not escape his attention. And I, for one, would have no wish to destroy the illusion that prompts her gift and that gives her solace.

What led to the increasing commercialization of so many Christian organizations? My next-door neighbour who recently became a Christian was bewildered at a missionary letter he received with a space at the bottom for him to indicate how much he might feel led to pledge.

'I didn't think real Christianity would be like this,' he explained. 'It's not that I don't want to

52

give. But this is no different from the begging letter from the community club.' Was he wrong in expecting Christianity to be different from the community club?

I admire my Christian business friends. I may not always agree with their views, but I do not question their integrity. If the methods they urge upon Christian bodies arise from their business experience, who is to blame them? Yet how can we fail to see that so many fund-raising techniques are Christian only in the sense that Christians have adopted them? In every other sense they are identical with the techniques of modern business promotion.

Advertising: information or manipulation?

Obviously I am leading in to many serious and important questions, the answers to which lie beyond the scope of this book. Advertising is not wrong. Persuasion is not wrong. Both become wrong either when the motive for using them is greed or when in using them we fail to treat human beings as human, ignore their dignity and view them as objects to manipulate. But the agonizing question business executives and Christian leaders face is, 'At what point am I beginning to be guilty of these things?'

Taken singly, many of the techniques I have mentioned have something to commend them. It is only when we stand back to survey the scene as a whole that we begin to see what is happening. We have become so competent in our commercial competitiveness that God has been replaced on our boards of directors. His photograph, with a suitable brass plate, is still prominently and respectfully displayed in our head offices. (He is not dead. He has retired.) But if we are honest, most of us place the emphasis where our faith really lies – in modern methodology.

We must face the fact that the methods we use often undermine faith in God. This is what Christian leaders and business executives should beware of.

There is a certain predictability about the results of mass advertising, provided it is properly carried out and its appeal correctly calculated. Mass advertising is an experimental science. It analyses the results of this or that technique. It takes into account the moods and preoccupations of people both universally and in different geographical areas and then exploits them.

Are teenagers uncertain of what others think of them? If so, perhaps they can be persuaded that their problem is bad breath or body odour and be induced to buy mouth washes or deodorants.

Advertising is a skilled, highly complex device whereby people are not only informed about a product, but induced to purchase it whether they need it or not. Careful on-going psychological and market studies continually update its methodology. Mass advertising pays off handsomely. It has revolutionized trade over the last one hundred years.

I do not wish to get involved at this point in a discussion on the complex sociological and ethical issues that mass advertising raises, but simply to note that many religious bodies have not been slow to make use of its techniques. They can be counted on even more than God can.

Advertising is not just persuasion. It also

includes information. No-one quarrels too much with information, provided it is *true* information. Tragically, Christian advertising does not always even inform accurately and sometimes depends on persuasion to an unhealthy degree.

A Christian organization that placed great stress on informing the Christian public of its activities adopted the following technique. A staff worker, following instructions from the head office, set herself a quota in personal soul-winning. Upon achieving her goal of six or eight converts in a month, she would instruct each to write a brief account of his or her conversion. The account would be edited and the convert instructed to memorize it, so that he or she in turn could bear witness readily and not be tongue-tied. A copy of the account would be included in the worker's next prayer letter along with a photograph of each convert.

In the above example I could look critically at several points, but for the moment I will focus on one point: information. Obviously the technique has superb advertising potential. A monthly letter from which six or eight faces smile their tales of conversion at you will hit you with a wallop. As you read it you say to yourself, 'Here God is indeed at work. This is something that merits my support.'

Yet in the words of one worker, 'The ink would scarcely be dry on the paper before most of the converts had ditched their "faith". This happened constantly.'

The information in the prayer letters was misleading. Though there may have been no intent to deceive, the fact was that the faces that smiled when the photographs were taken were no longer smiling. The stories that appeared in the letter were not the stories being told when the letter was read.

What led to the unintentional deception? Was there in somebody's mind too great a need to 'sell' the organization to the Christian public? Was the advancement of the organization a higher priority than the advancement of God's reputation? Did this lead to a lowering of the scriptural standards of truth? Was the whole thing just an elaborate sales pitch?

It did, in fact, reap superb financial returns which in the minds of many people meant that God was behind it. My own belief, however, is that we are viewing an example of the worship of money. And lest we hasten to reassure ourselves that our own methods are unimpeachable and that we would never countenance a scheme like the one I described, let me say that the details are irrelevant. What matters is what led to so great a need to sell a work to the Christian public. And this is something that involves us all.

Chapter Five

Christian competition

Let me, for a few moments, adopt an ungodly perspective. I will try to put God in the back of my mind and view Christian work from a merely practical standpoint.

The pressures to compete

Christian organizations work in a competitive climate. While gold is plentiful, there never seems to be enough of it flowing to maintain, much less to expand, all the existing organizations and churches, to say nothing of new ones. It follows that organizations compete for our money as well as for our prayers.

The fact is seldom discussed or even recognized. Mission leaders are aware of it because of the financial pressures they struggle under. Pastors are aware of it, especially pastors of 'live' churches, because of the flow of mail across their desks. You would be surprised to know how many organizations might want their representative to speak, however briefly, on a given Sunday morning from certain church pulpits. One hears the phrase 'If we can get him in *there*' frequently during discussions about the strategy of deputation.

Certainly since the Second World War a kind of covert guerrilla warfare has been fought out among older and newer Christian organizations. While organizations often form alliances and friendships, when the fate of the individual organization is in question, it is every institution for itself. Established denominations and some older interdenominational groups have money and prestige on their side. Solid downtown property, investments of other kinds plus complex annuity schemes give them a certain edge on the praying public's attention. Younger groups need to be (and often are) more aggressive to compete.

The war is the uglier because so few of us are willing to open our eyes to it. We pretend it does not exist. We have to, for we live with two irreconcilable ideas in our minds: the greatness of God and the facts of everyday life. So we gather together in certain associations, smiling our radiant smiles and giving warm Christian handshakes, all the time secretly assessing one another's potential as a competitor. We do not really understand that God can easily supply all our needs. We forget that we should be as concerned with our brothers' and sisters' needs as with our own.

The weapons of our warfare are prayer letters, magazine articles, straightforward advertising, public speaking, films, tapes. On the whole we fight cleanly (at least in public). We devote our energies mainly to promoting our own causes and not to destroying other people's. However, in private many of us are expert character assassins. We have to be when we see money going in the wrong direction.

Some results of the competition are bizarre. We have already seen that the people who are least competent to judge how money should be spent are too often the ones who actually decide. The people who have money to give seem, in practice, to control the direction of Christian activity. It matters little whether such people are big givers or small givers; the rule holds.

If we are dealing with small givers, it is admittedly hard to say who exactly controls whom. (Remember, we are leaving God out of the picture for the moment.) Advertising tends to influence small givers more than large givers. It follows that the work that gets financial backing from small givers will be the work that is best put across (in film, by personal presentation or however) or which has the most psychological appeal. A scheme to airlift missionaries by helicopter to remote tribal regions will generally get more financial backing than a similar scheme to evangelize down river by canoe. In this example the outcome may be unimportant. You need less money for canoeing than for a helicopter. And as for effectiveness in evangelism, who can say which scheme is better? As one experienced tribal worker put it to me, 'What a tremendous opportunity to spend four weeks in a canoe with a bunch of Indians. God really works in situations like that.'

But there are other times when the outcome may matter more. What it boils down to is that the people who have the least knowledge and expertise in Christian work, and who may be the least discerning, give to whatever project seizes their imaginations most.

Big donors need to be cultivated with individual skill. Just as top sales representatives fly first class to negotiate with state legislations, so top Christian leaders negotiate with very wealthy Christians. Some of the latter are discerning and have neither the wish nor the desire to control the direction of Christian work. They take very seriously their responsibility as stewards. But some feel that their wealth itself entitles them to control. They reduce principals of Bible colleges to a state of panic and mission organizations to a crisis of faith by displaying their angry disagreement with one thing or another. Do they secretly relish their ability to cripple a work by withholding their support? Perhaps they see themselves holding, as it were, a majority of the shares in the Christian enterprise.

I am generalizing and oversimplifying complex matters, but there is substance in my observations. What alarms most of us when we contemplate the scene differs greatly, however, from what bothers God. It is perhaps time we brought him back into the discussion.

We may grow alarmed at the thought that the control of Christian activity could sometimes lie in the hands of an immature Christian public and at other times in the hands of some opinionated Christian tycoon. It seems to us an unsatisfactory way of deciding what gets done and what doesn't.

Possibly so. But we are thinking as the world thinks. We see money as more important than it really is. Money is powerless to generate spiritual activity, and lack of money is powerless to cramp it. We have forgotten to listen to God's plans and have totally underestimated his power. We have assumed that misdirected money will thwart him. And so long as we think like this, we will be in danger of doing what so many Christian workers do: glorify God with our lips but bow down to money in practice.

Yet we must continue to look at the way Christian enterprise grows daily less distinguishable from business enterprise. As we do so our focus must not be on success (whatever that means) but upon the devastating effects the transition has upon the church's relationship with God and with the honour of his name. For remember, we are concerning ourselves not with the growth of the Christian industry but with the idolatry that underlies it.

Expansion and blessing

Commerce thrives on two principles: expansion and competition. 'You must never stand still,' the proprietor of a small business will tell you. 'Once you stop going forwards, you start going backwards.' Do the words sound familiar? Did you perhaps think they were Christian principles? If they are, they were first borrowed from business.

It is natural to want to expand an enterprise. Growth symbolizes success. All too readily the small Christian organization, delighted to have brought the gospel to a thousand people, assumes that it must strengthen its stakes and lengthen its cords. But expansion can take place at the expense of quality. And expansion can intoxicate us with the scene of glory ahead. David paid a terrible price for his egocentric head-count of Israel (1 Ch. 21). And somewhere along the line many Christian evangelists and churches have done the same. Nobody could tell you when or how it happened, but little by little the church becomes important in and of itself. It used to pray for revival because it longed to honour God. Now it prays for revival because attendance improves when there is revival. Spiritual principles become of importance primarily in that they foster expansion.

And the moment you set your sights on expansion, inevitably you find yourself competing. Some Christians see nothing wrong with this. One prominent Christian leader unabashedly told me that when he had been in business he had found that it was best to start a new business in the places where business was already thriving. In a similar way he felt he should start a new Christian group 'where the competition is best' – that is, where other groups were already working.

Paul's principles were different. He refused to build on another's foundation and preached instead where Christ had not previously been named. Yet again and again missionaries and Christian workers find themselves involved in competition rather than co-operation.

Stealing Mexican sheep

As a relatively green missionary trying to help Latin American students, I learned all too soon what Christian competition meant. One day in

Lima, Peru, I found myself praying and planning with a Christian Mexican student. He had received much help from me when I was associated with the International Fellowship of Evangelical Students, and now he felt the call of God to evangelize Mexican universities. His Mexican colleagues and I suggested he complete his degree (a few months away) before devoting all his time to student evangelism. My student friend stressed the importance of the venture's being truly Mexican with a Mexican board and, if possible, Mexican financing. Until finishing his degree he had agreed to act as an agent in Mexico for a Christian student magazine published in Argentina.

The next day my friend told me he had received a message to make a reversed charge phone call from Lima to a number in the United States where a prominent Christian leader, also engaged in student evangelism, wished to speak with him. I waited outside the phone booth as he made the call.

'He wants me to fly up to the States to talk with him,' he told me as he emerged.

'Will you go?' I asked.

'He will pay my passage both ways.'

'When will you go?'

'As soon as I get my tickets.'

I felt bewildered. 'What does he want?'

'He says he wants to help students in Mexico.'

'Did you tell him what you were doing?'

'Yes. He said, "Have those people got you to sign anything?" He asked me twice, "Are you sure you've signed no papers?" So I told him no, that I hadn't signed anything.'

I was shocked. Was the implication that only signed commitments mattered?

He looked at me, hoping I would understand. 'I want to do what is best for Mexico.'

'Of course, and if you feel God wants you to go, you must go.'

'Well, I'm not sure. But perhaps I should go and see what he has to say. He wants me to get to know their work and then see how I feel.'

I was too naive to believe what my mind told me was happening. I thought that nobody who was a Christian would see money (in the shoestring operation I was engaged in, telephone calls to the States or sudden trips there were unheard of) to contact a novice already engaged in one operation and try to capture him for another. Nowadays I would have no hesitation in squaring with such a student so that at least he could see the issues straight. As it was he went as a lamb, and as a lamb was led into a new fold.

Maybe God meant it that way. But I know God didn't approve of the way it was done. I cite the instance as a flagrant example of what happens constantly in Christian work though usually in a less flagrant manner.

If your response is one of incredulity or indignation you fail to understand. Expansion is unthinkingly accepted among western Christians as something good and desirable in itself. And by expansion I do not mean the spread of the gospel, but the growth of particular institutions. Expanding organizations come into conflict over money, territory and workers. At times mature thinking prevails, and groups co-operate and collaborate. But equally often, conflict results in the kind of competitiveness I just described, which is no less fierce for being referred to in pious clichés as 'a matter for prayer'.

So the operation gets bigger. If smaller groups get crowded out, maybe that proves that God has lost interest in them. They should have had more 'faith'. Just as in *laissez-faire* capitalism, so in the Christianizing industry: the law of the survival of the fittest must be the law of God himself. As new organizations come into being, the finances of older groups are threatened. It may be that a denominational missionary society finds funds are flowing to an upstart interdenominational society. Or again, a well-established interdenominational society discovers that its constituency is now more interested in newer groups.

Obviously some Christian groups feel the pinch more than others. Some denominational missions have large reserves of capital. Wherever the pinch is felt most keenly, there the battle rages most fiercely. And a battle it is. Behind the firm handshakes and ecclesiastical jocularity, a struggle for economic survival often rages, none the less deadly for being covert.

No-one really knows what the financial potential of Christianity is. Like a great golden cow, the Christian public itself chews contentedly as scores of hands grab greedily for her udders. She is not likely to dry up, for the meadows in which she grazes are lush with green dollars. But the milkers grow anxious.

Fancy footwork

Why is it that several Christian organizations (and many more for all I know) have placed their public relations in the hands of 'Christian public relations' firms? How can it be possible that an outstanding Christian leader will allow his prayer letters (and some of the rest of his public correspondence) to be submitted to a public relations expert to be vetted before they go out?

Once again, it is often a matter of support. Leaders of a Christian organization feel it has to project the kind of image that will not offend those who have given for years and that at the same time will 'awaken prayer interest' in a wider constituency. And image-projecting calls for professional skills. One Christian leader spoke to me of the 'pretty fancy footwork' needed to keep diverse supporting groups happy. A wrong sentence may cost a hefty sum.

The more I study Christian organizations, the harder it becomes to distinguish them (in their policies and methods of working) from commercial enterprises. The examples I have given are only a few, but they form part of a picture which convinces me that we revere our own creation more than we believe in Yahweh. Not all organizations are so bitten by the success bug as some I have described. Nevertheless, most have in some degree succumbed to commercialized methods of fund-raising.

Most send carefully worded begging letters plus postage-paid envelopes. Others pursue different sources of potential income. Is someone making a will? Then explain how a legacy to a Christian charity is not subject to taxation. Does a widow need security yet want to give to Christian work? An annuity scheme may be just the answer: cash for the Bible college, income for the widow. Is there a death in the family? Then why not ask friends to give to a Christian cause rather than give flowers? Who can argue against the logic of money 'wasted' on flowers when Bibles are at stake? (Who could argue against the logic of money wasted on perfume poured over Christ's feet when the poor were going hungry?) So Christian organizations, like dignified vultures, join the undertakers, the florists, the needy relatives in a stately dance for pickings around the contents of a satin-lined coffin.

I do not know whether to be amused or saddened by the double messages Christian groups send out. The first message is: 'God is with us in a big way. Climb on board while you have the chance!' The second message is: 'Something dreadful is happening. We're about to be shipwrecked on the shoals of financial need.' To get both messages across at the same time calls for verbal dexterity.

According to the begging mail which arrives on my desk, the church is in dire straits. God is apparently doing a terrific job through all the Christian organizations that write to me, but he has run into a financial crisis that threatens to undo everything. Last year he was saved in the nick of time because he himself prompted people to give. This year, it looks as though he might not be able to make ends meet. So we must trust God and rescue him at the same time.

A conference on filthy lucre?

How can we stop the tide? We live in the age of conventions. We congregate in large numbers to hear big-name speakers speak on important issues. Who will organize a convention where Christian leaders from all over the world meet to discuss the place of money in God's work, to discuss faith and the ethics of fund-raising? The problem is so widespread and so complex that I feel helpless when I ask myself what the solution is.

I would like to see greater minds that mine, leaders of experience and seniority, gather in Lausanne or any other suitable place to talk about filthy lucre. There might be fireworks, but there might also be fruit. Is it impossible that God should revive his people as far down as their wallets? Is it impossible for the Holy Spirit to show us how we may reform our principles and practices? For only if we gather together and face the issue squarely will anything be done.

Some experienced Christian leaders have already made their views known. *Eternity* magazine a few years back published an interview with Edward Hales, director of Field Services for the National Association of Evangelicals in the USA. Several vital issues were touched on in the report.

First in importance (to my mind) was the tension between the teaching of stewardship and techniques for fund-raising. Christian leaders have a duty to teach God's people both the responsibility and joys of giving. Such teaching has a spiritual goal. Its aim is not to raise money but to set Christians free from their bondage to money, to teach them the liberty of liberality and thus to increase their joy in the Lord.

Techniques for fund-raising have, on the other hand, a material aim. They do not ask, 'How can I help the Christian public find freedom?' They ask, 'How can I induce the Christian public to cough up?' The second question may have some validity, but it is of less consequence than the first.

Christian leaders both in churches and in parachurch organizations must ask themselves, 'Which concerns me more, economic survival for our work or spiritual freedom for God's people?' Tension exists between the two goals. It is impossible to be equally concerned with both, and one must take priority over the other.

A second point arises from the first. Church pastors are in a position to feel the pull of both goals. Concerned with both the economic viability of the church and the spiritual needs of members, pastors are asking a real question when they wonder whether they should be dominated by economic or spiritual concerns. If they are wise and godly, they will choose to teach not only a sense of financial responsibility to their flocks but also how Christians may find release from mammon. Pastors should not cease to be concerned about economic questions, but their prime goal will be pastoral.

The position is very different in what have been described as parachurch organizations (such as interdenominational bodies). Leaders of such groups have a split constituency. They are responsible on the one hand for the spiritual well-being of people who have become Christians because of their endeavours. They are also responsible to the Christian public to whom they look for funding. It becomes much easier under such circumstances to have spiritual concern for the first constituency while viewing the second merely as a source of income. For pastors, no such split exists. When they survey the congregation, they survey both the source of the church's income and the flock to whom they minister.

Parachurch organizations are thus exposed more than churches to the temptations of stressing fund-raising techniques rather than being primarily concerned with the spiritual liberty of the givers. It is in fact very difficult for them to have a deep and godly concern for the Christian public.

Some might ask, 'Should we not then question the validity of parachurch structures?' The question is huge and has been ably dealt with elsewhere. I would propose an alternative and more down-to-earth question. How may we, the Christian public, protect parachurch organizations from financial abuse?

Hales, in the *Eternity* interview, pointed out that in the United States the federal government has already become concerned and that legislation to control dishonest practices seems inevitable sooner or later. It will indeed be a sad day when government action replaces self-regulation on the part of God's people. But in the meantime some form of self-regulation could start among us.

Hales also points to three reports on the ethics of fund-raising, reports from the American Association of Fund-Raising Council, the National Catholic Development Council and the Christian Stewardship Council. All of these have valuable suggestions. Christian leaders in parachurch organizations as well as in denominational mission organizations would do well to study the reports.

On the other hand, the Christian public must become more sophisticated. Christians must learn to insist on adequate financial reports from bodies to which they give money. They must learn how to evaluate such financial reports and be aware that some reports conceal the amount of money spent on things like promotion. They must ask 'Exactly how much cash did the organization have in hand at the year end? How much money is spent *on doing the job* and how much on overheads?' An organization that spends fifty per cent of its income on keeping itself going should be scrutinized with care.

More important still, we must become more discerning about the goals of each organization and whether they are being fulfilled. How honest are the reports of work carried out? Is the organization doing what it says it is doing? We cannot guarantee that we will never be conned, and it really does not matter if we sometimes are. But at least we will be trying, by an increase in what Hales calls 'donorism' (seeking to protect the donor as consumerism seeks to protect the consumer), to provide some incentive for better financial practices among Christian organizations.

Of course, I could be less ambitious than suggesting an international conference. If you are a leader, why do you not convene a retreat in your Christian organization to hash such matters over? The subject is dangerous, I know. It would be better still if various Christian organizations could sign some sort of armistice or treaty to de-escalate the fund-raising race in a manner that would not upset the balance of power too much. But what is to stop a unilateral de-escalation of fund-raising? Would it be too risky? Do you fear that the finger of God might write, 'MENE, MENE, TEKEL, PARSIN' over your organization? Then face your fear.

Face it together before God.

I do not believe that the extension of God's kingdom is held up by lack of money. Yes, indeed, Christian organizations (both denominational and interdenominational) are under financial stress. Of course their workers live sacrificially, doing without many things the rest of us have. But the financial problem is spiritually peripheral. I believe underpaid Christian workers are as much the victims of Christian empire-building and of wrong ways of going about things as they are of callous indifference on our part. We have become slaves of Christian institutions rather than servants of Christ.

But there is worse to follow. For Lord Mammon is not content that we worship him, especially if our worship is only half-conscious worship. He wishes to reduce our God to someone who can be bought and sold at cut-price rates in a bargain shop, and his people to laboratory rats who can be programmed to become nothing more than mechanical followers of Jesus. The first of these we shall consider in chapter six and the second in chapter seven.

Chapter Six

Selling the sacred

Up to now we have been looking at some fairly straightforward forms of the exploitation of the Christian public. The Bible college that relieves old ladies of their savings is at least doing so for what it sees as a good cause. Annuity schemes may be spiritually questionable, but they do not constitute a *racket*, at least not in the popular sense of the term. The Bible-college staff do not usually line their pockets with the widows' savings.

T-shirts, pencils, car stickers

The Jesus-pencil/car-sticker thing belongs to a different order of spiritual obscenity. It is filth of a fouler kind. It has to do with the greed that fills one's wallet from the fears, the joys and the tenderness that bring God and man together. It is desecration.

But at once I hit difficulties. There are any

number of ways of defending a T-shirt from which 'I love Jesus' blooms from an adolescent girl. Are T-shirts not needed? Is it wrong to sell them? Is it wrong to make a profit on the sale of clothing? And whatever could be wrong with encouraging a teenager to advertise the fact that she loves Jesus?

But, I ask, who made the garment? Were they concerned with making an honest profit on the manufacture and sale of the garment? How did they feel about the blessed name of Jesus? Were they really trying to combine an honest living with a chance to honour the name of Christ, or were they opportunists, seizing the chance of making a few more bucks by exploiting a cheap and silly fad? If they were doing the latter, they were guilty of desecration, and we who buy or tolerate such T-shirts are party to their desecration.

We humans get desensitized quickly to things which horrify us. It happened to me with human bodies when I was a medical student. One day I stood for the first time with a knife in my hand beside a naked corpse on a marble slab. My first dissection. Opposite me stood a young Christian woman, also a medical student. We both took deep breaths in spite of the slight odour, and our eyes were wide and staring. I touched the cold skin covering the body and drew back my hand, gripping my scalpel more firmly. I looked at my partner's frightened brown eyes.

'D'you want to have a go first?' I asked unchivalrously.

'No, you first,' she breathed.

Yet within two weeks it was old hat. We could

even (and sometimes did) joke about matters which would make other people's hair stand on end.

One can get used to almost anything. And we Christians are so desensitized to desecration that we do not notice it even though it surrounds us. Part of our problem, of course, is that we hardly know what the sacred is any more.

Unmelted snow, framed by brown earth

While he never uses the word *desensitize*, C. S. Lewis in his book *The Abolition of Man* charges some modern educators with desensitizing children to things which ought to awaken respect, awe and reverence. Lewis sides with the ancient philosophers in asserting that the most valuable function of education is to inculcate in the young what he calls *ordinate* (appropriate) responses to creation, to the words and actions of people around them, to good and evil – indeed to every aspect of life.

'Until quite modern times,' he writes, 'all teachers and even all men believed the universe to be such that certain emotional reactions on our part could be either congruous or incongruous to it – believed, in fact, that objects could merit our approval or disapproval, our reverence, or our contempt.'[1]

He quotes Plato, who describes the well-nurtured youth as one

> who would see most clearly whatever was amiss in ill-made works of man or ill-grown works of nature, and with a just distaste would blame and hate the ugly even from

his earliest years and would give delighted praise to beauty, receiving it into his soul and being nourished by it, so that he becomes a man of gentle heart. All this before he is of an age to reason; so that when reason at length comes to him, then, bred as he has been, he will hold out his hands in welcome and recognize her because of the affinity he bears to her.[2]

A thousand years after Plato, St Augustine described virtue as *ordo amoris*, 'such a regulation of my affections that I shall render to every object an appropriate kind and degree of love, or hatred'.[3]

I remember walking with two friends across the English moors in springtime. Pushing through bog and bracken, we were suddenly surprised by a cluster of pine trees where the last of the snow lay unmelted, framed by brown earth and deep green clusters of needles, washed by golden light from a late afternoon sun. Two of us stopped.

'Oh,' I said, catching my breath. 'Isn't that incredible!'

'Beautiful,' my friend breathed, awe in his voice. 'Just beautiful.'

The third member of the party hesitated, staring with a puzzled expression first in the direction we were looking and then at both of us. 'What is it? What are you looking at?'

'Don't you see?'

'Only some trees and snow. It's very nice, but . . .'

Some people, disagreeing with Lewis, would say that no beauty existed and that our responses reflected nothing more than differences in our subjective feelings. To this I would make two observations. First, I am grateful for the response I experienced to the sight of the snow and the pines. I am richer and happier for that response, and I do not want to change places with my second friend whom I saw as blind to the beauty.

My second point brings us nearer to our subject. All Christians, whether or not we agree with Plato, Aristotle, Augustine and Lewis about ordinate affections, must agree that an encounter with God *should* awaken in us awe, reverence, worship and adoration. There is an ordinate response to God, and the person who lacks it, who is desensitized to glory, and in whom wonder and fear are no longer awakened, is greatly to be pitied. Such Christians remind me of an appalling encounter some of my colleagues and I had with a schizophrenic patient.

She was admitted to the hospital after finding her parents dead in bed as a result of a double suicide. 'Oh, dear! What did you do?' one of my colleagues asked her.

'I phoned the dentist.'

'The dentist?'

'To cancel their appointments. They couldn't keep dental appointments if they were dead.' The reply came with no emotion, in a quiet, singsong voice.

However we may explain the woman's response, we recognize that it was not *ordinate* to the situation. Most of us would have responded to a similar situation with shock, horror, profound dismay and grief. Not to respond in this way would indicate that something had gone profoundly wrong with us, as it had in fact in the patient I referred to. I listened, appalled and frightened, by the hollow echo of a personality that seemed to be living in the woman's body.

We can see by now that it is impossible to separate desensitization to the sacred from desensitization to divinity. He who does not tremble before the radiance of glory will be tone deaf to desecration. We must first be awakened to beauty before we are horrified by philistinism.

The source of reverence

I know of no more moving description of what I am calling an ordinate response to deity than the one found in Kenneth Grahame's children's story *The Wind in the Willows*. Mole and Rat have been searching all night for Portly, a lost baby otter whose parents are stricken with grief because they fear him drowned. At dawn the two animals encounter him on an island above a weir in the river. He lies sleeping between the sheltering hooves of the god Pan. I quote the section in full — not as a tribute to a heathen god, for Grahame had no such purpose in the passage. Rather, he was revealing in the allegory his own experience of reverence for God, and doing so with such exquisite sensitivity and insight that the passage remains a model of the ordinate response I am discussing.

'This is the place of my song-dream, the place the music played to me,' whispered the Rat, as if in a trance. 'Here, in this holy place, here if anywhere, surely we shall find Him!'

Then suddenly the Mole felt a great Awe

fall upon him, an awe that turned his muscles to water, bowed his head, and rooted his feet to the ground. It was no panic terror — indeed he felt wonderfully at peace and happy — but it was an awe that smote and held him and, without seeing, he knew it could only mean that some august Presence was very, very near. With difficulty he turned to look for his friend, and saw him at his side cowed, stricken, and trembling violently. And still there was utter silence in the populous bird-haunted branches around them; and still the light grew and grew.

Perhaps he would never have dared to raise his eyes, but that, though the piping was now hushed, the call and the summons still seemed dominant and imperious. He might not refuse, were Death himself waiting to strike him instantly, once he had looked with mortal eye on things rightly kept hidden. Trembling, he obeyed, and raised his humble head; and then, in that utter clearness of the imminent dawn, while Nature, flushed with fullness of incredible colour, seemed to hold her breath for the event, he looked in the very eyes of the Friend and Helper; saw the backward sweep of the curved horns, gleaming in the growing daylight; saw the stern, hooked nose between the kindly eyes that were looking down on them humorously, while the bearded mouth broke into a half-smile at the corners; saw the rippling muscles on the arm that lay across the broad chest, the long supple hand still holding the pan-pipes only just fallen away from the parted lips; saw the splendid curves of the shaggy limbs disposed in majestic ease on the sward; saw, last of all, nestling between his very hooves, sleeping soundly in entire peace and contentment, the little, round, podgy, childish form of the baby otter. All this he saw, for one moment breathless and intense, vivid on the morning sky; and still, as he looked, he lived; and still, as he lived, he wondered.

'Rat!' he found breath to whisper, shaking. 'Are you afraid?'

'Afraid?' murmured the Rat, his eyes shining with unutterable love. 'Afraid! Of *Him*? Oh, never, never! And yet – and yet – O, Mole, I am afraid!'

Then the two animals, crouching to the earth, bowed their heads and did worship.[4]

Anyone who has experienced the immediacy of God's presence will recognize at once the authenticity with which Grahame writes. And anyone who has experienced what Grahame describes carries deep within the embers of precious fire, praying those embers will never, never be put out, valuing more than all earth's treasures a memory and the awakened capacity to adore.

God has, of course, no *need* for our reverence. He does not feed on our awe and adoration. But he who is worthy that all creation bow before him crying, 'Holy, holy, holy is the Lord of hosts! All time and space are full of his glory!' knows that unless people are moved to utter such words from the bottom of their hearts, they will know neither what it is to be created human nor what joy and glory are all about. And he longs that we be liberated to know the full purpose of our creation, to know him and to enjoy him for ever.

Desensitized to desecration

Josephus in his *Antiquities of the Jews* describes how Cumanus, fearing a tumult in the temple during the Passover at Jerusalem, posted armed soldiers in the cloisters. On the fourth day one of the soldiers, perhaps inflamed by wine, 'let down his breeches and did expose his privy members to the multitude, which put those that saw him into a furious rage, and made them cry out that this impious action was not done to reproach them but God himself'.[5] On the surface, Jewish indignation seemed to be directed against a foul desecration of the sacred precincts and of the God who presenced himself there.

The incident is one of several desecrations of the temple that ancient manuscripts record. Antiochus Epiphanes erected an idol in the holy place. Years later, a Roman army set fire to the temple, defying Titus, who himself appears to have been distraught over the desecration.[6]

Jews were understandably appalled, reacting violently. And we can see at once that obscene gestures, looting, burning and the erection of idols in a place where the holy Creator condescended to dwell between the cherubs constitute an abomination.

Why these terrible acts of insult? Probably the pagans had never had an opportunity to learn reverence for Yahweh. In addition, the desecrators seem not to have been thinking about

81

Yahweh so much as aiming a calculated insult at Jewish national pride. When one man calls another 'a son of a bitch', he thinks not of the mother he maligns but of the man he wishes to enrage.

And if we look carefully at the Jewish responses to the desecrations, we discover that the insults had found their mark. Jewish anger was not over God's honour but their own. Pagans and Jews each dragged Yahweh into the argument as a means of getting at the other. For instance, the Jews accused Cumanus of having incited the ribald soldier to perpetrate his obscenity. It is clear from Josephus' description of the scene that they were out to make political capital of the incident. Their 'religious' indignation was a sort of political blackmail bereft of any real concern for Yahweh.

The pagans had never learned reverence for him. The Jews had forgotten what reverence meant, had forgotten the lessons of the burning bush, of the flaming mountain that could not be touched and of the earth that opened to swallow the sons of Korah. They had been desensitized, as we ourselves have been, to desecration.

A religion without reverence

Admittedly many desecrations are spawned by people who could not care less about the things of God. The boom in gospel music is largely exploitation of a popular mood by pagan business people. We cannot blame Christians for what pagan merchants do.

Again, making money out of religion is not in itself desecration. Servants of the gospel have to live by the gospel.

Therefore profits on Christian literature, tapes,

records, preaching do not constitute a desecration of sacred things. Rather, it is when greed sees the chance of a quick profit from those whose hearts have been made vulnerable by their yearning for God that desecration's ugly fungus is spawned.

I remember seeing once the transfigured face of a girl in an evangelistic meeting. She was kneeling and had suddenly looked up, her cheeks awash with tears. It must have been in that moment that the wonder of God's love had broken over her, for the expression of joy that shone blindingly from her was indescribable. For a moment I stared, fascinated. Then instinctively I turned away and bowed my head.

But supposing I had felt like capturing and exploiting commercially what I saw. Supposing I could have filmed that moment with the kind of magic that can transcribe emotion and use it to advertise an evangelistic technique I was perfecting, so that I would be asked to preach more widely – or just to make money. I never do so, of course, yet the same sort of thing is so much a part of the current religious scene that we do no more than shrug.

Why get upset about an 'I love Jesus' T-shirt? The Chinese never used to pronounce the word for God. It was too sacred. The word for heaven would take its place. The ancient Hebrews had similar feelings about the name Yahweh (Jehovah). As a Christian, I feel perfect liberty to pronounce the name Jesus. But if I pause to think when I pronounce it, it has a powerful effect on me.

I am reminded of a Creator who did not despise a woman's uterus, who allowed himself to be reduced to an infant so that he could fully share my humanity, who associated (though he was God) with poor peasants, who despised the horrors of death and sin, vanquished death itself and rose again. I know that one day at this same name of Jesus every knee shall bow. Can you ask me then how I feel when that same name is used as a gimmick to sell T-shirts? (And if you are naive enough to feel that the gimmick can be a 'witness', you should earn the difference between advertising and witness.)

You might argue that I have chosen something trivial that should be ignored. For a long time I would have agreed with you. Yet as I see the rage that the Son of God expressed against the money-changers in the temple, I know that the issue can never be a trivial one.

Ours is a religion without reverence. Other religious traditions have at least expressed contempt and disgust at the sellers of idols, at religious postcards, medals and other cheap junk. But where are the voices of protest here? The Lamb of God is reduced to bright pink on a car sticker.

Visit the Holy Land!

The same desecration may take many subtle forms, and Christians can be drawn into collusion with the money-makers. How, for instance, should we view Christian tours to the Holy Land? Pastors are involved as sub-agents of travel agencies. The pastor gets a free trip as a tour guide. Before long he or she may be making tours regularly and may even take a spouse along. The travel company benefits by the increased turnover of sales resulting from the pastor's Christian contacts. The pastor gets a change (by no means a restful one) in routine.

Once again the question may be asked, What harm is there in all this? We could go further. Are we not doing a great good by gratifying the longing of many Christian people? Will they not see the very places where our Saviour's feet have trodden? What an opportunity we are giving them!

What an opportunity ... Do the words sound familiar? They appear too frequently in promotional literature. Are we not in fact doing what some Roman Catholics have done around their shrines and cathedrals (and what other Roman Catholics have detested) all through the ages – merely desecrating the sense of the holy by commercial opportunism?

We have not sinned against the people who take the tours. We have certainly not sinned against the stones of Jerusalem, though we may have contributed to a semi-worship of them. Most of the tourists return with glowing eyes and burning hearts.

We sin against God by exploiting the financial potential of those glowing hearts. For the question has to be asked, Where does the interest of the tour promoters lie? In the glory of Jesus? In the happiness of his people? Or in the turnover of the ticket sales? A house of prayer can so quickly become a den of thieves.

A profit-spotting spirit

Commercial desecration, then, cannot be defined in terms of any specific form of religious commercial enterprise. It has to do with the spirit that too readily spots the profit potential in the longings of God's children. The heart is deceitful above all things and desperately wicked. Of the Christian publisher I ask, Which is uppermost in your mind, the needs of the church or a potential bestseller? I know we have to be practical. I know bestsellers can supplement the loss on some poorly selling book that has a needed ministry, but it is not of these things I speak. Rather, it is of the eye that spots a book which will pander to the credulity of the spiritually naive, that will cash in on the latest spiritual fad, that will be part of a boom. More than this I ask, Is your heart cold and cynical? Are you in it for the profit or for your company's growth potential?

And the same questions could be asked of organizers of Christian conferences and holiday centres, owners of bookshops and tape ministries, Christian property developers, pastors of growing churches. I cannot answer the questions myself. I only have a strong sense as I survey the whole religious scene (in North America particularly) that if Jesus were to come among us again, he would still find money-changers in the temple precincts and act as violently now as he did then.

What can we all do about it?

Well, the local bookshops would not suffer terribly if we boycotted stupid car stickers, Jesus T-shirts, Jesus pencils, bookmarks, praying hands, charismatic jewellery and such sacrilegious garbage. Why don't pastors call on their congregations for such a boycott? How about home-group discussions on 'Modern money-changers and how to overturn their tables'? How about a discussion on 'Commerce and tours to the Holy Land'?

The problem is that sacrilege cannot be defined. It arises both from spiritual colour-blindness and from callous indifference to the longings of those whose hearts seek after God. We therefore must examine our own hearts. We can ask ourselves whether we have been lured into the seats of the money-changers. We can ask God to show us the motives in our hearts in any matter where money has to do with the sacred person of our Lord and God. If the Holy Spirit shows us we are in any way involved in desecration, we can quit. There may be financial loss. There may be embarrassment. But there will be refreshment and renewal in our lives.

We are not ourselves called to plait a whip of cords. Our rage is not called for, only our repentance. Where we see (or where we *think* we see) desecration flourishing, we should pray both 'Spirit, convict' and 'Father, forgive!' Apart from this we must confine ourselves to not touching the unclean thing ourselves.

It has its roots in the worship of money, and we must smash the altars of money from our own hearts, our households and our businesses. Its worship dishonours the name of our God. And as we shall see in the next chapter, it strips the divine likeness from the face of his creature – man, male and female.

Chapter Seven

Evangelism abuse

I became a Christian as a child of eight. My conversion took place in a large marquee where an Irish evangelist preached an old-fashioned gospel. My two most vivid impressions are the smell of fresh wood shavings and the phrase 'substitutionary atonement'. I requested of my mother a definition of the latter, and when it was given, I remember saying without any hesitation, 'Well, then, I'm saved.'

No-one told me to 'witness'; indeed, I would not have understood what the word meant. Yet the day following my conversion I found myself telling my bewildered friends at school what had happened to me.

As the years passed, I attended many gospel services and campaigns. At first all went well. But the older I grew and the more I heard and saw of the preaching of the gospel, the more deeply my faith was shaken. Any 'worldly influences' I might have been subject to played little if any part in making me doubt. I grew well acquainted with Scripture, and in the religious instruction classes at school I frequently stood up alone and openly opposed the instructor's attacks on Scripture. So vehement was my opposition that I was asked to attend no more classes in religion but to spend the period in the school library. I did so, defiantly memorizing long passages of the New Testament.

Honest about life

The opponents of Christinity have never caused me to doubt. Only the preachers of the gospel sowed doubts in my heart by their apparent hypocrisy. I had a fondness for literature and read voraciously both modern and Romantic novels and poetry. Instinctively I began to see the relationship between truth and great literature. I could not at that stage have expressed the matter in words, but as in my mind I compared the evangelists I knew with Dickens, with Shakespeare, with Tolstoy and with Dostoyevsky, I felt instinctively that good writers were more honest than good evangelists. The comparison increased the questions in my mind.

My disturbance grew deeper as I began to take an active part in evangelistic campaigns. In the course of time I began to act as a counsellor and to encounter the kind of people who 'went forward' and 'made a profession' but woke up the next morning wondering what hit them. No amount of discussion with some of these persons served to convince them of the truth of Scripture or the reality of what had happened to them in the evangelistic meeting. In fact, the experience embittered them, leaving them with a deep hostility to the gospel that seemed impossible to quell.

For many years my feelings continued that something was profoundly wrong with modern evangelism. Manipulating people like rats or machines at times characterized the presentation of the gospel. The uncanny resemblance between evangelistic campaigns and sales campaigns undermined my confidence in what the evangelists said. So deep was my concern that at one stage in my life I was swept perilously toward permanent agnosticism. Only as I gained an understanding of the self-revelation of God in history and of the historicity of Christ's resurrection from the dead did I also gain a deep and quiet assurance that even modern evangelism could not shake.

Evangelistic manipulation

I do not accuse my fellow Christians of holding the view that humans are mere machines. I know only too well that they, theoretically at least, subscribe to the beliefs that humans have souls, that they have spirits and that they are responsible for their actions. This is why evangelism opens a more serious question about the way Christians view their fellow men and women. It is one thing to treat them as laboratory rats in order to open their wallets. It becomes altogether a more serious matter when we do so to psych them into the kingdom.

Does God sweep people into his kingdom by bypassing their minds and wills? To read some descriptions of revivals would lead us to think so.

Yet Scripture teaches otherwise. 'We have renounced secret and shameful ways; we do not use deception, nor do we distort the word of God. On the contrary, by setting forth the truth plainly we commend ourselves to every man's conscience in the sight of God' (2 Cor. 4:2).

It seems that Scripture consistently reflects the approach that I address myself *first* to people's understanding ('by setting forth the truth plainly') and *second* to their consciences ('we commend ourselves to every man's conscience in the sight of God'). If I am faithful in doing this I may discover that people's *emotions* are also affected and that their *volition* responds with decision and faith. But the order is supremely important: understanding, conscience, emotion, will. I must not appeal directly to emotions but to the mind.

Thus the revival described in Nehemiah 8 began with a reading and explanation of the Scriptures 'so that the people could understand what was being read' (Ne. 8:8). When they understood their error, their consciences were pricked and their emotions aroused.

Unfortunately, you can stir people's emotions without their understanding being enlightened at all. But only that stirring which springs from an enlightened understanding and a quickened conscience does justice to our true nature. Anything less insults us and dishonours God.

Brainwashed converts

One night when I watched a TV interview of an American businessman who had been brainwashed into signing false confessions in Hungary, I saw where the problem was. For the first time I began to suspect that what appeared to be Christian conversions might often be nothing more than brainwashing.

The thought that conversion may at times have no spiritual dimension but be exclusively psychological may seem shocking. Nevertheless it is a fact.

Conversion, of course, *is* a psychological phenomenon. *Psychological* means 'pertaining to the mind'; *phenomenon* means 'something that can be observed'. All conversions involve a change of mind and a change that becomes evident to others (and can therefore be observed). What distinguishes Christian conversion from all other types of conversion is that the former is accompanied by regeneration or new birth. Christian conversion occurs when the change in attitude is associated with a sowing of the living Word in the mind of the believer and the springing forth of a new life from God.

In some parts of the world (notably in China) western evangelistic techniques have been used to convert students to communism. Large student meetings were held in China following the revolution. Enthusiastic communist 'evangelists' harangued the crowds with the gospel according to Mao. Young communist converts gave popcorn testimonies. Songs were taught and sung. Emotional appeals were conducted, and ardent personal workers dealt with enquirers. As students yielded themselves to the new faith, the light of joy would break over their faces, and a new sense of purpose and commitment characterized their lives.

What happens in the emotional life of someone

who is converted (in a Christian or in any other sense)? We still have a lot to learn, but it would seem that prior to many conversion experiences people grow increasingly anxious and tense and may feel profoundly guilty. At a point where the distress reaches a peak, they suddenly experience a radical change in their orientation to life and goals. At the same time they are suffused with relief and a profound sense of peace and joy.

My purpose here is not to discuss technical psychological laws but to point to dangers of which most Christians are unaware and to show how the commercialization of Christian activity has been partly to blame.

Anyone who knows how can produce conversions. They need not be true Christian conversions, but they will be real in the sense that the person undergoing the phenomenon will experience revolutionary changes in his or her feelings and outlook. For anyone so heartless as to try the experiment, the rules are as follows:

1. *Make people anxious.* You can do this in a number of ways. One way is to make frequent changes in the noise levels of the room. It is now well established that changes in perceptual input create anxiety. If you are speaking, try yelling at the top of your lungs, and then dropping your voice to a menacing whisper. It doesn't matter too much what you say at this point so long as you use your voice properly. Use singing and musical instruments in the same way. Amplifiers can help greatly. The important thing is to work up to a crescendo, and then let the sound sink into a velvety silence punctuated by soft but clearly enunciated syllables such as, 'And . . . this . . . my

friend . . . is . . . what . . . may happen to you.' Let the silence go on for a few seconds, and then begin immediately yelling at a decibel level slightly higher than your previous crescendo. Many of the people listening to you will find that their under-arm deodorants have stopped working, their mouths are dry and their pulses have quickened.

2. *Induce guilt.* Most people spend a lot of mental energy keeping guilty thoughts at bay. So inducing guilt is not difficult once you discuss a few sins with the volume modulations that I described in Rule 1. Speak as one who knows. Or better still, tell your audience that God knows about the dirty little thing that is festering in the minds of so many present. Once you've got them anxious, it is fairly easy to make them guilty. Repetition is valuable at this point.

3. *Destroy their judgment.* This is more difficult. The best way is to switch frequently the *emotional tone* of the meeting. If you are good at weepy stories, tell one as skilfully as you can. Then grow solemn and try the up-and-down volume technique. Sound as though you're angry and indignant. Talk about the awful calamities that are coming on society: war, earthquakes, pollution. Then instead of doing the velvety silence sequence, tell them a joke. You'll be amazed at the response. It has nothing to do with your skill as a comedian. It is only an index of the anxiety present. They are laughing from relief at this point. After this, go back to something weepy. Before long your experimental rats will have lost touch with all the normal bearings by which they know what is what, and you will find that many of them are putty in your hands.

4. *Repeat the same cliché over and over again.* It doesn't really matter whether they understand what you're saying or not. At this point you are communicating on a non-verbal level anyway. It's the rhythm and the emotional tone that are getting through more than the content. Some Christian evangelists find it very effective at this point to get the choir to sing very softly. Any faint moans from the converted will help create the mood you're striving for. And whether it's money, dedications or professions of conversion that you're after, all you have to do is pull in the net.

5. *For camps and conferences you should encourage exhaustion.* Communists have found this effective when dealing with prisoners. Emotional and physical exhaustion, especially when associated with lack of sleep, helps to weaken any resistance to the brainwashing process.

Am I being heartlessly cynical? Am I perhaps making a mockery of the Holy Spirit's power? Not at all. I am exposing some contemporary practices. For in our spiritual harlotry we are conceiving children, but too often they are bastards who will never inherit glory.

Made a machine?

That non-Christian totalitarian states should manipulate people to promote their interests surprises me little. But that Christian organizations, proud of their belief that people are free moral agents made in the image of God, should treat them like laboratory rats appalls me. I can only wonder at such a dichotomy between our professed beliefs and our overt actions.

You may ask me, 'Is there no place for emotion

in preaching?' Obviously there is. I do not protest against emotion but against its artificial manipulation. Sometimes when I preach I find it hard to suppress my tears. The preacher who understands the solemnity of his message has something to weep about. But I would sooner have a weeping preacher and a dry-eyed congregation than a skilful preacher who is personally unmoved, save by a joy in his or her capacity to make the congregation weep.

My atheist acquaintances may smile at this point and suggest to me that manipulation pays off. When we treat people like machines, they respond like machines; therefore, they must *be* machines.

In this book there is hardly room to do justice to the point. It is true that our central nervous system has many of the qualities of a computer. It is also true that many of our *actions* seem computer-controlled. When you sit on a pin, you jump. No rational decision, carefully weighed and considered, precedes your leap from pain. The action is mechanical. And so is the energy you automatically feel when your bloodstream is flushed with adrenalin.

If you had to figure out what to do every time you sat on a pin, your conscious life would be cluttered with trivia. In fact, some forms of mental illness consist of precisely such a cluttering. I see patients sometimes who are obsessed with whether they should carry a handkerchief in their left-hand trouser pocket or their right-hand trouser pocket, and whether the handkerchief should be changed five times a day or six times a day. They are no longer free to live, to love and to enjoy the glory of life.

Human beings are, of course, made in the image of God. This is what gives each of us our infinite value. To treat people like things, like machines (even if they respond like machines), is sin. It is contrary to God's entire purpose for the world, which seeks to lift each of us to the full glory he originally planned.

A bearer of news

I call, therefore, not in my own name, but in the name of the sovereign Christ of God, upon anyone who presumes to regard himself or herself as a preacher of the gospel to have done with preacher's tricks. I don't care how wide your radio or TV coverage is or whether you preach in a tiny frame building in the slums. Your first job as a preacher is to *inform*. You are a bearer of news. It is news that must be explained clearly and in detail. There need be no journalistic tricks to play on sensational angles. Let us have done with tabloid preaching. Let us also have done with pandering to popular fads and fashions. (Once it was communism. Then it became the joys of sanctified sex techniques.) The good news is that God became man, lived, taught, died and rose. He is now glorified and will come to judge the world in righteousness.

The Holy Spirit can touch people's consciences only if their minds have been enlightened with clearly enunciated good news. Truth is for the mind, not the emotions. Your first job is to inform the *minds* of men and women with *facts*. If you do that, the Holy Spirit will awaken their consciences. Only when people's consciences are awakened by the Holy Spirit can their emotions properly be stirred. And even then God will stir them only by awakening them to the true gravity of their condition and the wonder of Christ's love. Such awakening, such stirring, is God's part, not yours. Your job is to *inform*, not to dabble with wills and emotions.

And the same applies to you who are not preachers. Your job, likewise, is to inform your colleagues of plain facts. To explain them. To show their relevance. Christ is not a product to be marketed, nor are those to whom you witness customers.

The great god Science

How could we have drifted so far from a biblical view of evangelism? What has seduced us away to 'win converts' in ways that contradict the very gospel we preach?

Not only has our materialism led us to worship money. It has also walked us down the centre aisle of the temple of the great god Science, where we bow before his laboratory-coated priests. We have more respect for archaeology, psychology, psychiatry and sociology than we have for the Scriptures. Do we not rush to say, 'The Bible must be true *because science has proved it*'? But what are we saying? We are saying that science is the ultimate authority.

Why are we so anxious for science to confirm the Scriptures? Is it not because we have more confidence in the 'assured findings of modern science' than in the Word of God, so that we feel ill at ease with the latter until the former has come to its rescue?

And nowhere does our worship of science

prove more disastrous than when we pay heed to its view of the human race. Let us pause to look at the confusion our idolatry has wrought in our attitude to our fellow men and women.

Materialism is a theory that says we live in a universe which has nothing 'outside' it, a universe which has always existed. Randomly moving particles cause other particles to move. The universe, if not a gigantic machine (lacking the precision and uniformity of machines), is yet related by complex chains of cause and effect, and what appear to be laws that account for everything that is and that happens.

Part of the system is humanity itself. It is important to grasp this. Humans are not the controllers of or even observers of the system, but an integral part of it. Materialism, taken to its logical conclusions, asserts that we cannot make decisions (though we all think we do). We are programmed like computers. If our behaviour seems complex, it is merely because of the complexity and sophistication of our programmes.

Such a concept of humanity is full of problems, a discussion of which lies beyond my present purpose. All I wish to emphasize now is that to the materialist, people are not capable of logical 'thought' or 'decision'. We have no will of our own. If we knew the details of the programmes, we could predict every word and action. We are robots. Our emotions can be turned on at the touch of psychological buttons. With sufficient understanding we could (and can) be made to laugh or cry like toy dolls.

This doctrinaire form of materialism (about which I will say more in chapter eleven) says matter is all that exists. Pragmatic materialism, on the other hand, teaches that matter is all that matters.

Our actions and attitudes are valuable if they contribute to producing and accumulating things. Many governments are pragmatically materialistic. When they say, 'The greatest good for the greatest number of people,' they are thinking of cars, homes, jobs, clothes, medical care and so on. Most middle-aged parents think this way too.

But notice. On the surface it looks as though we who admit to being pragmatically materialist at least honour human dignity and worth. Yet closer examination shows that this is not the case.

The catchphrases of pragmatic materialism are 'Get a good education and you'll get ahead', 'Money talks', 'Money isn't everything but it can make life a whole lot easier'. Materialism sees national well-being hitched to the rising star of the Gross Domestic Product.

You may say, 'At least we are concerned with human well-being.' But we are talking about human dignity, not human well-being. How, for instance, do we go about 'improving the well-being of people'? We do so at the expense of their dignity. We subject them to media manipulation so they will buy what we want them to buy, wear what we want them to wear, eat what we want them to eat. Whatever we may profess about believing in human dignity, our actions betray us. We base our commercials on theories that assume people are either laboratory rats or computers. We then proceed to strip them of dignity in order to load them with things.

I have suggested that many Christian groups

contradict their profession of valuing spiritual things more than physical. Their approach both to life and to their ministry is commercial. Christians who pride themselves in possessing life eternal often appear to live by the rule 'Seek ye first the kingdom of money and, with careful budgeting, many fringe benefits will be added unto you.' Our actions and our beliefs do not match.

Take, for example, Christian begging letters. I have already indicated that experience has taught experts how to open someone's wallet. People are more likely to give if you enclose a prepaid envelope and a deed of covenant form. The letter (or booklet or folder) must arrest their attention. It must be easy to read. It must make them see how much you appreciate their interest, how important their contributions will be. In a word, it must psych them into giving. You adapt your method of begging to human responses. The 'angle' you work on in your advertising is the one most likely to produce the response you are after.

Commercial enterprises describe the method openly and unashamedly; Christians squirm uncomfortably or else indignantly justify their begging techniques. 'How can you call it begging when what we are doing is encouraging people to experience the blessing of giving to God?' My answer remains, Which concerns you more, the blessings for the people who get your begging letter or their responses in your return post? In using commercial gimmicks to raise money, you are treating Christians the same way as behavioural psychologists treat trained rats. By worshipping the great god Science you show not only your lack of confidence in God but also your contempt for humanity.

Origin, identity, owner

As we re-evaluate our approach to evangelism, allow me to introduce three important themes that I will take up again in chapter nine – whence we came, who we are and to whom we belong.

Whence we came. When I look at a colleague at work, hardened in his sin and unbelief, it sometimes seems impossible for me to see how he could possibly become a Christian. So wide is the gap between our ways of thinking, so self-assured and at ease does my friend seem, that my prayers die on my lips. Even God could not arouse such from darkness.

I am walking, of course, by sight rather than by faith at this point. I am believing in the visible more than in the invisible Holy Spirit. Nevertheless my dilemma is a real one. A hopelessness has descended on my soul that seems impossible to shake off. Unless . . .

Unless I could somehow get him to a meeting where . . .

Unless I could somehow get him to read . . .

Unless I could introduce him to . . .

What is wrong with my reasoning? It is wrong simply because it reveals that I can believe an invisible God will work only *if I can see some visible means by which he will do so*. I can believe if my friend will come to the meeting. If not, I really don't see how. And this is the point at which idolatry begins.

You may say, 'But it's not in the *preacher* I'm believing but in the God behind the preacher!'

And that is exactly what idol worshippers say. 'It is not the piece of stone we believe in, but the god behind it.'

Don't get me wrong. I too preach and write and meet people. But you would be turning me into an idol if you believed God would save your friend only through my instrumentality or through some similar visible, understandable device. So long as seeing is believing, believing is still unbelief.

Were you a likely candidate for salvation? Yet didn't God save you? And while he may have used some human instrument, don't you see that he would have saved you with or without any instrument? And haven't you seen other 'impossible' brothers and sisters delivered likewise by the incredible power of the invisible God?

Do you realize whence you came? You were in the grip of hell. Demons had wrapped their chains about you. The god of this world had blinded your understanding. Yet God struck off your chains and the face of Christ illumined your soul. The damned around you are no more damned than you were, their chains no thicker, their darkness no deeper. Nor is the power of Christ to save them one whit less.

Our modern evangelistic methods display our tragic unbelief in the power of God because we have already forgotten the pit from which all of us alike were dragged by divine power. Therefore we have to rely on methods that work, that is, whose working we can see.

Who we are. We are children of God, not children of science. Science can explore only the fringes of God's laws. We are not in the business of pseudo-spiritual brainwashing. We do not belong among experimental psychologists or the pathetic ranks of sales armies.

We are the followers of the Lamb. We tread in the footsteps of apostles and martyrs. We gauge the success of our preaching not by the number of our converts but by its clear adherence to the truth. We are those who are to be filled with the Holy Spirit. We would rather be laughed to scorn and thrown to the lions than descend to gimmicks and trickery to turn on a crowd at an evangelistic meeting.

We are clothed in garments of salvation. Angels and demons look on to see what we will do. We bear the mark of God upon our foreheads. We are citizens of heaven, future judges of the universe, fellow heirs with Christ. Let us beware lest we forget the high dignity of our calling.

To whom we belong. We belong in practice to whomever or whatever gains our open allegiance. We owe our allegiance to Christ. None of us would deny it. But the essence of harlotry lies in looking to other sources for what our true bridegroom gives us freely.

And what will he not give? Does he not now sit at the right hand of God? Has he not told us that all authority in heaven and earth lies between his fingers? Is he not the author whose writing creates the history enacted before our eyes? Has he not sent his Spirit? Is the Spirit not even in this moment working in the minds and hearts of millions who as yet have heard no word of Christian testimony? Did he or did he not rise from the tomb? Did he or did he not make the sun stand still, open the waters of the Red Sea, cause the walls of Jericho to fall with a trumpet blast? Has he not for twenty centuries created revivals, reformations and awakenings without any mechanical aid that we could devise?

And do we or do we not belong to him? The question is a solemn one, for in my ears I hear querulous voices of the future pleading, 'Lord, did we not organize rallies in your name and in your name bring thousands to the exhibition hall? Lord, did we not put on a television show that brought in thousands of dollars for your cause?' And for some of these the answer will be, 'Depart from me, you workers of iniquity, into outer darkness. For I never knew you.'

Let us turn then to Christ himself. In the chapter that follows we shall try to understand the fury of his assault on the commercial desecration of the temple.

Part two: Following other gods

Chapter Eight

The prophet's whip of cords

He made the whip himself (Jn. 2:15). Therefore his act of enraged violence was premeditated, not an impulsive outburst. He made a plan and he carried it out. Seizing tables piled with coins, he tossed them on their sides. An uproar of protesting and excited voices was heard amid crashes of heavy furniture on stone, tinkling of rolling coins, and the swish and crack of his whip. The bleating of sheep and the lowing of oxen drowned out the muted sounds of the frightened pigeons.

Whether or not the whip bit deep into the flesh of human shoulders we do not know, though I suspect it lashed down on people as well as on animals. Some translations read that he turned over the stools of the pigeon sellers, and as likely as not he unseated some by doing so. They would lie sprawling as the panicked animals stumbled over them.

The miracle is that protests were as feeble as they were vain. He would be sweating and panting with exertion, and there would be a calm purposefulness in his eyes that people could not face. Sheep, oxen, pigeons and people (who would snatch up whatever they had time to) were forced amid the hubbub through the gates.

Still, having done so much, he did not yet stop. Unsuspecting merchants arriving with more animals would be startled to find their way barred and a whip gripped in the menacing fist of the man with the unflinching gaze (Mk. 11:16).

It is false to assume that there was something supernatural about the awe he created. Though he was God, he called down no legion of angels to help him, nor is there any evidence that a mystical terror paralysed the merchants. His control of the crowds was by a moral force, forged by his total lack of ambivalence and the money-changers' uneasy consciences. He was expressing what the common people deep within their hearts had known for years.

Like some modern clergy and academics who bleat inane polysyllables from pulpit and ivory tower, the religious authorities tried verbally to browbeat him. He dismissed them with a riddle. In their dismay, they promptly began to plot his death (Mk. 11:17–18).

Again and again, both in the driving away of people and animals and in his teaching to the crowd, the words recurred, 'How dare you turn my Father's house into a market!' (Jn. 2:16). And waxing stronger, 'Is is not written: "My house will be called a house of prayer for all nations"? But you have made it "a den of robbers"' (Mk. 11:17).

110

Few sermons are preached on the incident. We ourselves, as it were, stand among the crowd silent and disconcerted.

The enraged Christ

Commerce has flourished on the skirts of religion from time immemorial. And our day is no exception, as we have seen in the last six chapters. It is time to consider what God's response might be to our waywardness. That is my theme in this and the next several chapters. To begin, then, let me ask, At what was the Son of God enraged?

It is an important question. In a life marked by gentleness and compassion, this incident alone shows Jesus as a man of violence. Friends and foes alike were awed and bewildered. And since this is so we must assume that such a divergence has unusual significance. The source of his rage must lie in a more flagrant evil than any other he encountered. His previous verbal outbursts against the Pharisees were hardly gentle. But only on this occasion did he resort to violence.

What was it about the traffic in coins and animals that offended him so deeply? 'A house of prayer' he had called it, not a place of teaching nor yet a place of sacrifice. (He himself was to be the sacrifice.) What was in his mind?

It is interesting, as Alan Cole points out in *The Gospel According to St Mark*, that what enraged the priests and Pharisees was so different from what enraged the Son of God.[1] Both they and he might be said to have had reverence for the temple. But though priests and Pharisees were scandalized at the desecration caused by the noise of the children, they apparently saw nothing amiss with the

111

commercialism in the courtyard. There is evidence that the high priest may have owned some of the stores ransacked by Christ. Certainly the system flourished under the protection of the temple hierarchy.

And why not? The money-changers were performing a service for the worshippers. People journeyed to the temple from many lands. Since temple dues had to be paid in Tyrian coinage, a convenient exchange had developed for travellers with foreign currencies. Were the money-changers not entitled to make a profit? How could they live if they performed the service gratis? What if a little cheating did take place occasionally? Was that not human nature? Can it ever be ruled out entirely?

Do we in the West share the outlook of the priests rather than that of Jesus? What do we say when small children run laughing and chasing inside our church buildings? Do we say, 'Hush! This is God's house'? (If so, we teach them a lie. God does not dwell in buildings of cement and steel, any more than in pseudo-Gothic show-pieces. His people are his dwelling place.)

The priests' idea of reverence was perilously close to respect for themselves, for their religious system and all they, in the pomp of their positions, thought they stood for. They would have been shocked had you told them they no longer stood for Yahweh and his name. But you would have been telling the truth. They were guilty of idolatry. The dignity of the buildings was what mattered to them.

A place of prayer. In the purposes of God, the temple was to be a place in which all nations might

112

have access to him. Isaiah's prophecies must have
been in the mind of Jesus as he cleansed the
temple. In their spiritual declension the Pharisees
and Sadducees had lost true reverence for God.
And though it hurts me deeply to say it, many
churches in the West seem to have no reverence
for him either. Arrogantly, we worship our own
institutions, our buildings, our programmes. It is
a sick and devilish worship for these things to
reflect our glory, beaming our egocentric worship
back upon ourselves to exalt us in the eyes of the
world and of our religious competitors. We have
become gods in our idolatrous religious empires.

The prophet Christ

Jesus was consumed with passion. Nowadays we
have forgotten how to see him as prophet. He was
God the Son, deity incarnate. He was man,
sharing both our human estate and our human
condition. He was our representative, our substitute, our sacrifice. He is now our compassionate
High Priest. He is our Lord, our king, the captain
of our salvation, our shepherd, our bread of life.

But prophet? Sure – *prophet*, priest and king,
but . . . We find it hard to think of him as prophet,
so accustomed have we grown to seeing him in
other terms. And as we view the details of his
earthly ministry, we unconsciously remove our
'prophet' spectacles, seeing him as teacher, healer,
fisher of persons, the unrecognized Messiah, God
the Son, the Son of Man approaching Calvary
with purposeful, unhurried steps. Perhaps we
grow uneasy since to see him as prophet is to see
him as some of his contemporaries saw him – *mere*
prophet.

Yet he was the last great prophet, the greater-than-Moses prophet. He was the ultimate prophet who conferred gravely and in transcendent glory with his predecessors, Moses and Elijah, on the Mount of Transfiguration. He was the final member of the long prophetic line.

And whatever its unique characteristics, his ministry stood squarely in the prophetic tradition. He addressed the word of the living God to the sinful, faithless leaders of God's people. The crudeness and violence of the old prophetic language became, in the prophet Jesus, violent action in the very centre of religious life. Like the prophets who preceded him, he fearlessly defied established authority in the name of Yahweh.

To understand Jesus the prophet, we need to understand the prophetic tradition he stood in. He charged the Pharisees with idolatry in the same way as the prophets of the Old Testament charged Israel with it. To bring their condemnation home, these ancient men of God accused the nation of prostitution. The people of Israel had sold themselves repeatedly to other gods even though their true spouse was God alone. The allurements of political security, social acceptability and economic advancement had wooed them often to beds of defilement.

Time has a way of mellowing the past, even of lending it charm and beauty. The stern denunciations of the prophets and the violent action of Jesus in the temple stir us only in the way pictures in an art gallery do. We view them with wondering eyes, marvelling that such dramatic power, such beauty, can exist; yet as we pass into the hubbub of the streets, we leave the pictures

114

behind. But if the prophets were to step out of the pictures or if Jesus were to leap, whip in hand, from the pages of the Gospels to confront us, how would we respond?

There is an uncanny similarity between our day and that of ancient Israel. God's ancient people worshipped Baalim; we worship money. At the heart of many of us is a greed for things. We have made the world's agenda of status-seeking our own. Unquestionably we have adopted the world's techniques of gaining influence and security. And it has worked. We are flushed with success. We take pride in the many celebrities who are Christians – athletes, musicians, politicians and more.

Not long ago we in the West were noted for our political clout and the empires of our tele-vangelists. Now the former is diminished and the sins of the latter have brought the empires down. How much more failure will we yet see in our ranks? Like the flower of grass fades human glory. Would that we anchored ourselves to God's unfading glory.

God weeps over our sins. He grieves over our waywardness. He yearns for us to realize that there is no place for two treasures in our hearts. He seeks to win back his bride who has found another lover. It is time to recognize what we have done and to repent of the sins into which we have fallen.

Chapter Nine

The prophets' whip of words

Accusing God's people of harlotry was a startling way to call attention to their sins. But this is exactly what the prophets did. When we look at the passages where they do so, we become aware that more than name-calling is involved. Ezekiel, for instance, accused Jerusalem of being a prostitute. But did you ever hear of a prostitute who paid her clients to do business with her? That's what Ezekiel accused Jerusalem of doing (Ezk. 16:31–34).

I ask the question for two reasons. First, it reminds us that when the prophets called Jerusalem a whore, they may have been using the word as we might ourselves. We know what a whore is. When we call someone a whore, we feel we know what we are talking about. But second, the issue at hand is not what *we* think when we use such distasteful words but what God thinks.

If we were to turn for a definition of harlotry to sociology, or even if we were to lug from our bookshelves our largest and heaviest dictionaries and encyclopaedias, we could have a good, perhaps even a salacious, discussion. But much of what we might say would be beside the point. I take my hat off to the learning of sociologists and lexicographers, but when we look at something from God's perspective their learning may not help, for they do not concern themselves with the prophets.

Many hundreds of years have passed since the prophets of God thundered their denunciations against Israel's and Judah's whoredoms. When they raised their voices they did so because God was displeased with his people. To be sure, he was displeased in particular ways and about particular things. Hence the inspired and metaphorical use of the term *whore*. The real issue, however, is not the technical appropriateness of comparing prostitutes and religious institutions, but whether God is displeased with his people – displeased, that is to say, in the same ways he was when the prophets charged Israel and Judah with whoredom.

Our starting point, then, must be with the prophets. Why did they speak thus? What had so enraged God? What did he have in mind in comparing his people with those involved in sexual immorality?

Let me return to the whore Ezekiel described. Her absurd discount rate raises a question. To take a loss on your business means you are pretty desperate to stick with it. Jerusalem may not exactly have loved her lovers. Prostitutes seldom do. But when they do, they become desperate

117

indeed. Ezekiel is assessing a wretchedness which implies an inner spiritual sickness. While he alludes to certain sinful practices in Israel, he is more concerned with the condition of the heart that gives rise to them than with the practices themselves.

Isaiah, Jeremiah, Ezekiel and Hosea all tell us something about the whoredoms of God's people, though Ezekiel and Hosea have more to say than the other prophets. Ezekiel utters a beautiful allegory about the foundling whom God made his bride, but who betrayed her divine husband. Hosea's relationship with his promiscuous wife gave him, at the cost of great personal pain, the profoundest insight into God's attitude to his people. Looking to the prophets for a definition of a whore – a definition, that is, of what constitutes spiritual whoredom – we find unexpected answers.

If we look carefully at the contexts in which such words as *whore*, *whoredom* and others are found, we shall gain a substantial part of the answer. Scholars may rightly add certain footnotes to what we decide, but the main thrust of what the prophets say seems clear enough. And as we read, we should consider how God might consider us as well.

Sons, asses, oxen, harlots: Isaiah

When, for instance, Isaiah talks about Jerusalem's whoredom (Is. 1:21–23), his specific charges concern the adulteration of precious metals and the watering down of alcoholic beverages. He goes on to accuse Jerusalemites of bribery, corruption and murder. The people of his day, then, were guilty of commercial dishonesty (exploitation of the consumer), legal corruption and violent oppression.

As we look at the wider context of the verses, however, we see that God uses other metaphors to express his grief over his people's sins. They are children rebelling against their father (Is. 1:2). They are worse than oxen, which at least know their owner, and donkeys, which at least respond to their master (Is. 1:3). Rebellious sons, stubborn asses, forgetful oxen and an unrighteous harlot – all four images describe how God sees a people who have forsaken social justice.

These metaphors have one point in common, the theme we considered in chapter seven: God's people, in sinning as they do, have forgotten *who they are and to whom they belong*. The ox and the ass behave as though they were their own masters. The son denies his filial duty.

We might ask why the prophet does not simply state this. Why does he not put it in plain language? 'God is shocked at your corruption, your violence, your exploitation. In behaving as you have, you have forgotten who you are and to whom you belong.' What could be more effective in awakening people than bold, plain speaking?

I suggest he uses the image of harlotry for two related reasons: Israel's relationship with God could aptly be compared with a sexual relationship, and the word *harlot* had in itself a shock value.

What feeble things words are! Or, to put it more accurately, how clever the human heart is in resisting them! The problem with Jerusalem's populace then is the same as that with many Christians today. They were busily religious.

119

They crowded the temple courts with their sacrifices, oblivious to their inconsistencies, serenely unaware of Yahweh's grief and rage (Is. 1:12–15). God therefore selects the most stinging word that could be chosen to shake his people from their complacency: 'How the faithful city has become a harlot!' (Is. 1:21). *Asses* and *oxen*, yes. *Sons* – that word, too, is altogether acceptable. But *harlot*! The word is offensive, shocking.

Let me pause a moment to draw a conclusion, a conclusion we can test as we look at the rest of the prophets. The Holy Spirit's inspiration of terms like *harlot*, *whore* and *prostitute* is designed to sting people into shocked awareness that their sins (whatever those sins might be) enrage God because his people have forgotten *who they are and to whom they rightly belong*.

If what I say is true, then you see what a waste of time it would be to fuss over a precise definition of the word *harlot*. To us, what makes a prostitute is sex for cash. We distinguish prostitutes from other sexual sinners in that whereas some people 'do it for love', prostitutes 'do it for money'. We even use the infinitive *to prostitute* metaphorically. Artists talk about prostituting their art when they produce inferior works to please the populace or purely to make money. We must be careful, if I am right, not to fall into the trap of imposing our own ideas of prostitution on the prophet's use of the words. Isaiah used the term *harlot* to sting people into realizing they had betrayed their identity and their loyalty. Let us look at the other prophets to see if they used the term in the same way.

Crude but effective: Jeremiah

Jeremiah is crude and graphic as he speaks of Jerusalem's harlotry. Repeating Yahweh's own words he writes,

> 'I will pull up your skirts over your face,
>   that your shame may be seen –
> your adulteries and lustful neighings,
>   your shameless prostitution!
> I have seen your detestable acts
>   on the hills and in the fields.
>
> (Je. 13:26–27)

Horror and contempt are obvious. Jeremiah seems to be finding the most scathing expression available to goad Jerusalem.

But what sins does he label harlotry? Throughout the book he refers to different failures. In the immediate context Jeremiah refers to the fact that Judah has gone a-whoring after other gods. Idolatry is the sin he has in mind.

Moreover, if you look carefully at the verses quoted above, you will notice not one but several expressions, all referring to the same sins: 'your adulteries and lustful neighings, your shameless prostitution . . . your detestable acts.' He piles one phrase on another in an attempt to emphasize how wretched, how shameful Judah's behaviour had been. Word studies are hardly necessary. To play with the etymology of the passage would be to do what C. S. Lewis described as trying to see fern seed while remaining blind to an elephant standing ten yards away. What comes through overwhelmingly is God's reprehension for what

121

his people are doing.

It would seem possible, then, to apply the same principle we discovered in Isaiah. God's people have forgotten *who they are and to whom they belong*. The chosen people, the privileged possessors of the Law and of the mercy seat, are fooling with petty little demons. They are violating their covenant relationship with God, oblivious to their heinous offence of forgetting the Most High.

Bribing your lovers: Ezekiel

Ezekiel's treatment of the theme is lengthy, moving and full of allusions to Jerusalem's history. In Ezekiel 16 the city is portrayed as an infant abandoned at birth, rescued, brought to full womanhood, espoused, cleansed and clothed as a princess by the Most High. God has no reason to pity so despicable and unattractive an infant, yet he treated her with royal grace and kindness.

She became a harlot by worshipping idols and by making military alliances with Egypt, Assyria and Chaldea. Forsaking the true God for false gods, she placed her trust in powerful neighbours rather than in the arm of the Lord. Vividly Ezekiel describes the shameful exposure and humiliation that await her, but hints at the end of the chapter at an ultimate redemption and restoration.

Just as the other prophets did, Ezekiel uses the term *prostitute* as a lash, not as a precisely defined word. It appears many times in the chapter before he eventually clarifies it. 'You were unlike a prostitute, because you scorned payment,' Ezekiel says to Jerusalem.

'You adulterous wife! You prefer strangers to your own husband! Every prostitute receives a fee, but you give gifts to all your lovers, bribing them to come to you from everywhere for your illicit favours. So in your prostitution you are the opposite of others; no-one runs after you for your favours. You are the very opposite, for you give payment and none is given to you. Therefore, you prostitute, hear the word of the Lord!' (Ezk. 16:31–35).

Two things are clear. First, the word *prostitute* in Ezekiel's day meant what it means today. He spells out the details explicitly. At the same time he makes it clear that he is not concerned with the precise commercial negotiations by which people of his day (as well as of our own) might define prostitution, but with the horror of the betrayal of a sacred relationship.

But notice, second, the difference between God's perspective and our own. If we were to set up a scale of sexual virtue, most of us would place prostitution lower on the ladder than adultery. Both are sins, but prostitution seems to belong on a lower rung. Adultery is bad enough, but in the back of our minds an excuse suggests itself. At least the adulterers may have cared for each other. It was not a cold commercial contract where a body was sold for sex.

If we read again the passage from Ezekiel, however, we see that it overturns our standards. It is as though Ezekiel were saying, 'A prostitute at least works for pay. But you are worse than a prostitute. You actually pay lovers to come to

you.' To us the greater evil is the commercialization of sex. To God it is the treachery, the
ingratitude, the violation of a holy relationship,
and its chief shame is the need to solicit and to
purchase from inferior sources what a holy God
has always given freely.

And when we remember that the one who so
offends God was once a filthy baby lying abandoned in the desert, how much greater the offence
becomes! Jerusalem's harlotry grieved God
because when she committed it she forgot who she
was, *whence she came* and to whom she belonged. It
follows that whenever we forget the same things,
we are on the brink of spiritual harlotry.

Ezekiel makes it clear that God is a God of
passion. Jerusalem's treachery did not leave him
unmoved or indifferent. 'Then my wrath against
you will subside and my jealous anger will turn
away from you; I will be calm and no longer
angry. Because you did not remember the days of
your youth but enraged me . . .' (Ezk. 16:42–43).
It is left to Hosea, however, to give us some sense
of the range of God's feelings towards a treacher-
ous spouse.

In love with a harlot: Hosea

Hosea married a harlot, Gomer. Whether or not
she was a harlot by trade before Hosea married
her is not altogether clear. But there was a serious
question about the paternity of their first three
children. Gomer eventually left home and ended
up for sale in the slave market, where Hosea pur-
chased her; he took her back home and treated
her with restraint, firmness and kindness. He tells
us little of the turbulence of his own feelings, but

124

his subsequent prophecies show that his experience with Gomer opened his heart to an understanding of God's attitude to Israel, the harlot whom he sought to woo back to himself.

The Holy Spirit often makes us aware of God's attitudes and feelings by causing us to pass through deep waters. I well remember an army officer who years ago attended the Keswick Convention in Britain, an annual event encouraging Christian commitment. With a bet of £10 he claimed he 'could go right through Keswick unscathed, untouched'. Beneath his bravado was an aching emptiness. One night after conversing with him I found myself weeping bitterly in the fields, overwhelmed by sorrow at his helpless plight. He seemed to be a cork, passively tossed about on cross-currents of ideas, with no ability to control the direction he was moving in.

I do not often weep for others, nor am I inclined to react emotionally to conventions, yet there seemed no bottom to my sorrow. Suddenly in the darkness I had a strange sense of the Lord's presence. It seemed he was saying to me, 'I see your little pool of sorrow. Why do you not let it flow into my great ocean?' It was the first time I saw and felt something of the immense compassion of the Saviour, so much so that my grief was turned into worship. I am glad my friend's restoration was delayed long enough for me to make my own discovery.

We can only imagine some of Hosea's intense grappling with bewilderment, despair, rage, revulsion, jealousy, love, pain, tenderness. Had God actually commanded him to marry Gomer?

Could God be the source of such pain and tragedy? What did God want him to do now that she had abandoned him? '"Go, show your love to your wife again, though she is loved by another and is an adulteress. Love her as the LORD loves the Israelites, though they turn to other gods and love the sacred raisin cakes." So I bought her for fifteen shekels of silver and about a homer and a lethek of barley' (Ho. 3:1–2).

If Ezekiel was made aware of the terrors of divine judgments against Jerusalem's harlotry, Hosea became aware of more. To him was given a vision of God's unending tenderness to the bride of his choice through experiences he himself underwent. From his own pains and joys he could bear witness to God's mercy by prophetic utterances of unusual insight. More than this, he was a flesh-and-blood example to Israel of enduring faithfulness in the face of perfidy. He became, if I may use the expression loosely but reverently, the faithfulness of God made incarnate in the eyes of his fellow Israelites.

Hosea gives the fullest and most complete picture of God's attitude in the face of harlotry. Once again we find terms like *harlot* and *adulteress* used synonymously and interchangeably. Harlotry is in fact defined as 'forsaking the LORD' (Ho. 1:2, RSV). A careful reading of the book will confirm the basic principle I've already repeated: we commit harlotry by violating *who we are, whence we came and to whom we belong*. It matters less *how* we violate these things than that we dishonour God by doing so.

Hosea also makes us aware of the passions and reactions of a holy God, just as Ezekiel does.

Ezekiel spoke of rage. Hosea speaks of compassion and tenderness.

> 'Therefore I am now going to allure her . . .
>   and speak tenderly to her. . . .
> I will give her back her vineyards,
>   and will make the Valley of Achor a door
>   of hope. . . .
> I will betroth you to me for ever;
>   I will betroth you in righteousness and
>   justice,
>   in love and compassion.'
>   (Ho. 2:14–15, 19)

God is indeed a God of passion. But how are we to understand his feelings? Words like *jealousy*, *rage* or *tenderness* convey images to our minds based on our human experiences. This in itself may not constitute too serious a difficulty, for we are made in the image of God. Nevertheless, there are dangers in assuming our emotions are identical to his.

How could they be? We are fallen: he is holy. We are finite: he is infinite. We are in time and subject to change: God inhabits eternity and is immutable.

I will leave to those more competent than I the questions that such considerations raise. Obviously they are immense, and perhaps no-one here on earth can resolve them completely. But of two things we may be sure. First, in considering the feelings of God we are treading on holy ground. We must remove our sandals and walk softly with heads bowed low, ready to fall on our faces if need be. Second, while we may not fully understand what it means to say God feels, the Holy Spirit himself reveals to us that he does.

His feelings exist in relation to us. His jealous rage and tenderness burn against Christians guilty of idolatry, guilty of holding material things in higher regard than God. We do well to tremble lest we forget who we are, whence we came and to whom we belong. For our God is a God of fire.

Chapter Ten

The prophets and the shame of nakedness

The God of the prophets seems harsh and sadistic when he threatens his harlot bride. 'I will pull up your skirts over your face that your shame may be seen' (Je. 13:26). 'I am going to gather all your lovers ... against you from all around and will strip you in front of them, and they will see all your nakedness' (Ezk. 16:37). 'I will take back my wool and my linen, intended to cover her nakedness. So now I will expose her lewdness before the eyes of her lovers; no-one will take her out of my hands' (Ho. 2:9–10).

Where do the prophets gain the notion of so crude and indecent a form of punishment? Does it reflect the culture they were part of? Were harlots so treated in Judah and Israel in their day? Would a betrayed husband normally act towards an erring spouse in this way?

The answer to these questions is no.

Certainly terrible penalties might fall on a harlot's head. A priest's daughter who prostituted herself might be burned to death (Lv. 21:9). Other prostitutes might be stoned (Dt. 22:21; Jn. 8:5). But shameful public exposure is mentioned only by the prophets, and even then only in relation to God's people. To my knowledge, there is no evidence that harlots were ever so treated. It is possible that a harlot sold in a slave market might have been exposed to display her desirable attributes to lascivious buyers. But this would not be punishment. It would be social abuse.

Let me put the matter another way. Let us suppose that Jeremiah, Ezekiel and Hosea wrote as they did because of what they had seen. In that case, why do they never mention in their prophecies burning or stoning – the customary fates of harlots under the law? We must conclude that the exposure so consistently threatened by the prophets had little if anything to do with how harlots of their time were punished. Each prophet in his turn, inspired by the same Spirit, wrote of God's dealings with spiritual unfaithfulness. Stoning might be appropriate for the physical sin, but public exposure was to be the fate of the spiritual harlot.

The language is crude and graphic. Had only one of the three alluded to the matter, we might have dismissed it as unimportant. Yet as we read what each has written we almost get the feeling that they had met and reached a common agreement, so closely do their words and ideas coincide. Yet we know that no such collusion ever took place. The shocking notion of a harlot's being stripped, mocked and exposed to the contempt of her lovers is inspired by the Spirit of God. It refers to the fate of his people.

We must therefore ask why so crude a measure was to be adopted. Was God being malicious? Or was there some strange blend of justice and healing in his terrible and shameful sentence?

Naked and ashamed

We humans are ashamed when we are naked. (There are exceptions to the rule – exceptions which, if we examine them closely, reinforce it.) To be naked is to be ashamed. In nightmares we find ourselves on the street or at work or in church partly or completely unclothed, struggling to conceal ourselves in any available crevice. Our nightmares reflect our underlying terror of exposure.

The shame seems to be confined to human beings. Animals and birds may be ashamed if we disfigure their coats or their plumage. But in so doing we are not denuding them, but interfering with the form of their bodies. The shame they feel may be related to our shame of nakedness but is not the same. Some dogs slink around with their tails between their legs if certain parts of their anatomy are trimmed. But this is no different from the reaction of a naval friend of mine who became unpopular on our ship. His colleagues shaved off one half of his beard and the other half of his moustache. His hairy face had been his pride and joy. Its gross disfigurement was a source of humiliation and shame.

And to be sure the element of being different from what we are accustomed to, different from the way we like to see ourselves, is part of the shame we feel at being naked. But it is only a part, and by no means the most important part.

The specific human shame of nakedness has to do with sexuality. Divorce sexuality from nakedness and its shame diminishes greatly or may disappear altogether. People who live in nudist colonies (for whom I offer neither defence nor apology) know this. People who do not live in nudist colonies fail to comprehend it, because in their minds sex and nakedness cannot be altogether divorced. A simple example of the separation of sex from nakedness would be that of getting undressed for a medical examination. For some people it is embarrassing, for others not. But the fact that the situation has (or should have) no sexual overtones reduces the shame of the exposure.

Our shame of nakedness is likewise a part of our fallen condition. The original pair knew they were naked after they had sinned. They hid. After their pathetic attempts to cover their bodies, the Lord himself mercifully clothed them. The shame of nakedness and the need for clothing were born on that day.

Whether or not their shame had sexual overtones is not clear. The sacred narrative makes no allusions to sexual relations before the Fall, but mentions them explicitly after it. Sin did not *produce* sexuality, but sin clearly made a change in its expression.

Of course there are people nowadays who display their bodies publicly on beaches, in movies, at nightclubs or in sexual orgies. In most cases the exposure is sex-related. It defies shame, sometimes for the sexual titillation of observers and for the financial profit of the exhibitionist. It is shame*less*.

But shamelessness in such cases is extreme sickness. It is sin carried (in a sexual area) to its utmost limit. A certain degree of shame about one's nakedness is healthy. To lose one's shame is to become less human. God did not respond to Adam and Eve's shame by telling them not to be silly, but by covering their shame. We are to be clothed.

Anthropologists might point out that some savage tribes live naked. I do not know all naked savage tribes, but I know some. I also know that nakedness to us is not always nakedness to them. A string, an ornament, an arm band, a decoration – symbolic perhaps, but terribly important to the wearer – signifies clothing.

We may assume then that our shame of nakedness, an attribute of our fallen condition, is essentially sex-related. As we read the prophets this must be doubly obvious. In exposing the body of the harlot, God is doing something explicitly sexual. He is exposing her lewdness, her abomination, her harlotries. It is this, in fact, that makes the retribution so harsh, so terrible.

Exposed and known

We humans are strange. In addition to the need to remain clothed and covered, we have an equally deep need to expose ourselves. The exposure can be precious, enrapturing and holy within the bonds of lifelong marital commitment. It is not primarily a sensual experience, though sensuality plays a part. Rather, it represents the hunger we feel to be known and accepted as we really are for our naked, secret selves. A hunger likewise to know, to reach out to another being and end the isolation and the aloneness for which neither of us was ever designed. ('It is not good for the man to be alone', Gn. 2:18.)

Life under God is not to be lived in isolation but in relationship with another. To be isolated is not to be fully human. But the drive to expose and to be exposed has dangers. In its proper place it is a gateway by which we dimly perceive God's relationship with his people. Misplaced or misused, it becomes a scourge – destructive, deadening and alienating. Its delights can turn poisonous. Its end can be cold disgust.

Physical strength was given to us to build, to protect, to guard and uplift the young and the weak. Yet the same strength can be a cruelly brutal scourge, murdering and pillaging the defenceless. In the same way our sex-linked drive to expose and to be exposed can be either a blessing or a curse to us. It has to do with a most sensitive area at the core of our beings. Its potential for the deepest human satisfaction gives it an equal potential for bitterness and pain. It can lead to human fulfilment but with equal ease to emptiness and cold despair.

So we are driven to expose as well as to clothe ourselves. I must not, of course, leave you with the impression that sexual relations make a marriage. A marriage based solely on eroticism is doomed to fail. We live in an age of genital athletics, of ecstatic achievements. They have to do with techniques. Technique at best is but a poor means to a great end and at worst a poor means to a worthless end – sensual delight for its own sake.

It is not to such things I refer. Rather, I speak of the purpose of exposure, that of knowing and being known.

With good reason the first account of sexual relations in the Bible was translated at one time, 'And Adam knew his wife.' For the purpose of sexual exposure is to accept and to be accepted: to accept another as he or she is and to be accepted as I truly am, to love and to be loved, to be faithful and to know fidelity, to be bound in a physical and emotional bond to which two persons commit themselves till death do them part.

Yet even the most satisfying marital relationship can never meet our deepest needs. Something within us cries for more – not for more sex or even for more closeness in human relationships, but for that which human closeness awakens in us, the hunger that makes us human and different from animals. 'For thou has made us for thyself', wrote Augustine, a millennium and a half ago, 'and our hearts are restless till they find their rest in thee.'

When Adam hid, he hid from God. Yet he and his descendants have ever since, whether consciously or not, yearned to dare expose themselves to God again: yearned, yet feared exposure to the Most High; yearned for the closeness for which they were created.

Israel knew a little (not much, but a little) of that closeness. God had revealed (exposed) himself to this people, and they, in fear and trembling, to him. But the covenant had been violated, the intimacy outrageously betrayed. The hunger in his people remained. In their folly they looked elsewhere to satisfy it, ignorant of the blasphemous obscenity they committed. They played the harlot.

135

We may take it that as a general rule the more sacred the trust, the more terrible is its betrayal. We are shocked, for instance, to learn of a mother who murders her baby. Cynical as we may be, it troubles us when presidents betray their countries for personal ends. To let someone down about a minor matter, say, to forget a dental appointment, is trivial. To break a promise to help someone in need seems more serious. If, for example, I solemnly swore to you to take care of your children in the event of your death, it would be treachery for me to abandon them to their fate and to ignore my solemn commitment. For this reason the betrayal of the trust within which it became possible for a man and a woman to disclose themselves to each other becomes a terrible matter.

It would seem to follow logically that the public exposure of such a sin should be correspondingly shameful. Yet so cynical is the age we live in, so jaded our appetites for the sensational and the horrific, that the mere disclosure of the facts of betrayals has begun to pall. We eat the news of a movie star's latest switch of partners with our daily bread. We drink presidential corruptions with our coffee. And though exposure by the media may be embarrassingly painful to the person exposed, it hardly affects the rest of us. Even a pastor's affair with a church member fails to bring us to our knees. We swallow it with relish.

Yet however cynical we may become, there is something about physical exposure that reaches all of us. I do not suggest it as an appropriate course of action, but if the erring pastor and church member were displayed *unclothed* before us, we would no longer react with relish but with profound shame.

A friend of mine who spent his childhood in Alexandria, Egypt, described a quarrel between a young Arab boy and his mother. Children and adults alike began to turn and listen as the two voices were raised in anger. The boy's fluency in vituperation, profanity and obscenity gave him an advantage. Suddenly the woman in exasperation raised her skirts and exposed herself to the boy as well as to the crowd.

'Look!' she cried. 'This is where you came from, and don't you ever forget it!'

A silence which could be felt fell on everybody in the street, and most of all on the shame-stricken boy.

God's honour, Israel's shame

Judah and Israel were to experience this same quality of shame. Not only they but the onlookers – the nations around with whom they had 'committed adultery' – were to be shocked into an awareness of God's standards and God's concern. The exposure was to have exactly the kind of effect on surrounding nations as the Alexandrian woman's action on the crowds. For God's own honour was at stake. Israel's shame was not only a punishment for her but a testimony to the world, a witness to the standards of a holy God.

We in the modern church confuse witness with reputation. We conceal facts discreetly, saying, 'It wouldn't be a very good testimony if this sort of thing got around.' Discretion is valuable in its place. What we sometimes forget is that the world around us is well aware of what goes on in our congregations and institutions. Truth will out. And as people begin to realize not only that our standards of behaviour are no different from theirs but that we tolerate and conceal what we profess to abhor, our preaching becomes an empty parroting in their ears. It is not sin which destroys our witness, but concealed and tolerated sin. If we were to deal with sin more openly, more radically, and to be less concerned with our reputations, our witness would in fact be powerful.

And among our chief sins, as I have already indicated, is that of our materialism. It has invaded us as a cancer eats out the inner vitals of a living body. It must be dealt with by radical surgery. If we do not expose it to be cured, then to be sure God will.

If we fail to deal with sin, God himself may have to deal with it publicly, so the world may know that he exists and that his standards remain unchanged. He may shock the world and shame us by revealing our nakedness for all to see. We shall cry in sickened dismay as we vainly try to cover our blushing faces or to turn our heads to one side.

Chapter Eleven

Treasure and heart

For many years, we lived in a materialistic world divided by iron and bamboo curtains into two materialistic camps, those of capitalist materialism and of communist materialism. To Christians in the West the communist variety seemed infinitely more sinister. Under western materialism the church flourished and religious groups were not only free but enjoyed tax concessions. Many churches were full. Superbly prepared literature grew in volume and sales. A missionary movement on an unprecedented scale has carried the Christian gospel to all parts of the earth.

Yet volume is no substitute for quality. In the other half of the world, where Christians were much less affected by the temptation of our kind of materialism, we found evidence of a spirit and a joy (in spite of suffering) which made western Christianity seem hollow.

Christians in China, in Russia, in Eastern Europe, in Africa, in Cuba lived lives of incredible heroism and bore witness with gladness. Though they were beaten, imprisoned, vilified and fiendishly tortured, their joy rose unquenchable and their faith stood unshakeable.

We make a mistake when we glibly assert that what the western church needs is persecution. We must be grateful for our freedom. The real explanation of the difference between underground churches of the East and showpiece churches of the West has to do with materialism.

The transition from communism to capitalism in Eastern Europe during recent years surprised us with its ease. Looking beneath it all, however, we see why: the communists, who were already materialists, simply adopted the capitalist form. Communist materialism is doctrinaire and oppressive. Capitalist materialism, which I earlier defined as the idea that matter is all that matters, is pragmatic and cancerous.

Many people who would never consider themselves to be materialists in the strict sense of the term nevertheless live as though material things were of supreme importance. My definitions are rough and ready, and my general statements are oversimplifications. Nevertheless they will serve my present purpose, for I am not writing a sociological treatise.

My definition of western materialism might appear to exclude Christians. No Christian would agree to the abstract proposition that matter is all that matters, for our very faith negates the assertion. Yet if our behaviour (as distinct from our verbal profession) is examined, many of us who call ourselves Christians begin to look more like materialists. We talk of heaven but we strive for things. Even so, Christians are rarely happy as materialists. Heaven tugs at us too vigorously. We find ourselves apologizing for our new cars or our larger houses. This tug of war renders most Christians ill at ease and at times ineffective.

Occasionally you may come across Christians who pursue wealth successfully yet who show no evidence of this struggle. I would say either that their financial success is coincidental – that is to say, they find it immaterial whether they make another million or not (for there are some millionnaires who do not care a fig for money) – or else that their Christian profession is false. In the latter case, they experience no heavenly tug in their hearts.

The misery of a Christian torn between heaven and material things can be pitiful. A self-made Cantonese importer invited my wife and me to dinner once. His house was breathtaking – a fortress outside and all softness and luxury within. In the foyer stood an artificial tree, perhaps five feet high, whose leaves and flowers were exquisitely fashioned from clusters of semiprecious stones. Ornate cabinets displayed valuable treasures. His tableware looked like solid gold, but we did not dare to ask.

Our host was about sixty years old and displayed a considerable knowledge of Scripture, yet as he talked there was no glow of joy about him. He told us he planned to make enough money to spend his closing years in serving the Lord 'without being a burden on anybody'. (The tableware alone would have kept some of us going in Christian work for quite a while.)

141

He never did get to serve the Lord. He had sold his heritage for stone and metal trinkets inside a painted fortress. He would have agreed that spiritual things matter more than material security, but his behaviour contradicted his professed beliefs. Riches had coiled like a living vine around his heart, slowly strangling his love for God and people.

Christians disagree about what the New Testament teaches on riches and possessions. Down the centuries there have been disproportionately wealthy Christians and others who have embraced voluntary poverty, giving away their possessions to serve God and their fellow human beings. What does Christ teach?

The social climate

If we are to interpret accurately Jesus' teaching about material wealth, we must have some idea of the social context in which he spoke about it. Dick France discusses the matter in *Third Way* magazine.

> The socio-economic situation of the time of Jesus is vividly illustrated by several of his parables. They reveal a sharply class-structured society, with landowners, stewards, tenant-farmers, day labourers and slaves. It was a situation in which the few could dress in purple and fine linen and feast sumptuously every day, while beggars sat at the gates; where capital steadily accumulated in the hands of the rich, while the ordinary free man lived under the threat of slavery for debt.[1]

France quotes an estimate that because of the double burden of religious dues and Roman taxes, a total taxation of about forty per cent would be exacted from an average income, *not* including unjust exactions of local tax collectors.[2]

Two things interest France: the social background of Jesus and his followers, and the chosen lifestyle they adopted. The social background appears to have been middle-class. Joseph, the earthly father of Jesus, ran a carpentry business and might even have employed workers. Matthew was a tax collector. Peter, James and John had shares in a boat and fishing equipment for their fishing enterprise. They, too, may have employed extra hands. Other followers included the wife of Herod's steward and women who 'provided for them out of their means'. Joseph was far from wealthy (indicated by his offering of two turtle doves rather than a lamb at Jesus' presentation at the temple), but he was a long way from being at the bottom of the economic ladder.

The lifestyle Jesus adopted, and which he encouraged his disciples to adopt, involved a renunciation (or at least a forsaking) of any private property other than the clothes they all wore daily, and a dependence on God to supply their needs through the generosity of the people to whom they ministered. They received food and lodging on their journeys, may have been more especially indebted to people such as Lazarus, Martha and Mary, and probably received gifts of money from time to time (though there is no record of their ever soliciting funds).

What they possessed they seemed to share in common, Judas taking care of the distribution.

From their meagre resources they probably still gave to the poor. (The protest against the waste of the ointment poured on the Lord's feet implies that giving to the poor was their practice; Jn. 12:4–5.)

Their chosen lifestyle raises a number of questions. Was it intended to be a model for all followers of Jesus? Was it perhaps a model for 'full-time workers'? Are there two classes of followers of Jesus, those who forsake all and live a hand-to-mouth existence as they serve him, and those who supply such workers from their capital and income?

There can be no question that during the New Testament period Christians adopted no universal economic practice. Many early Christians sold their goods and shared with others in the church at Jerusalem. It does not seem to have been expected that the practice should be universal.

Many scholars suggest that the generous sharing in Jerusalem was occasioned by the hardship of those who had come from a great distance for the Feast of Pentecost, had been converted and had stayed on. Others point to the probable poverty of even local converts. The action of the Jerusalem church is often criticized by modern Christians, who feel that the subsequent appeals to other churches would not have been necessary had the rash generosity of the wealthier Christians been more temperate. It would have been better, they feel, to have been less generous and to have encouraged more industry.

Yet is it not possible that we fear having to share our own resources with Christians in need? Where in the modern world do we find the kind of love and generosity which makes church members sell homes and cars that the hardships of other Christians might be met? Are there no local economic hardships among God's people? If there is no suggestion that the Jerusalem pattern should become universal, neither do the Epistles utter a breath of criticism of the Jerusalem church. When funds were being raised across Asia Minor and Europe to continue to help the Jerusalem poor, it seems to have occurred to no-one to blame the situation on economic mismanagement.

There is no doubt, however, that both among the early followers of Jesus and in the epoch of the New Testament church there existed two economic patterns. To quote France,

> Some of Jesus' followers were, and remained, rich and influential men. Joseph of Arimathea does not seem to have felt the need to sell his estate, despite sufficient commitment to Jesus' cause to impel him to defy the Sanhedrin and make a risky appeal to Pilate. Zacchaeus made drastic donations and restitution, but was not apparently required to renounce all his possessions.[3]

We could add other New Testament characters like Titus and the Philippian jailor and Lydia the seller of purple. On the other hand, Paul (with the exception of his occasional tentmaking) and his followers seem, like the apostles, to have largely opted out of the economic struggle.

To the question, Was there then a two-tier

system of discipleship under which the most fully committed who travelled with Jesus renounced private possessions while a wider circle retained their possessions and so provided the means for the support of the inner circle? France replies, 'To a large extent this seems to be the case: there was a distinction between the commitment of those who joined Jesus on a full-time basis and those of his supporters who remained in their homes and jobs.'[4]

France's reply leaves me uneasy. Are there indeed two kinds of commitment that Jesus calls for – even that he tolerates? Certainly no such idea is found in his teachings. 'If anyone would come after me, he must deny himself and take up his cross daily and follow me' (Lk. 9:23). 'Anyone who does not take up his cross and follow me is not worthy of me' (Mt. 10:38). The claims of Christ on his followers are expressed in various forms, yet always they seem to apply equally to every follower.

Nevertheless, there does appear to have been then as now, in economic terms at least, a two-tier system. In this France is right, though he himself points out that the distinction was far from absolute. Peter retained his property in Capernaum (Mk. 1:29) and returned briefly to fishing (Jn. 21:3). It seems (from a comparison of the account of his call and that of the post-resurrection fishing) that he retained his boat and equipment.

Yet commitment in economic terms is surely a reflection of commitment in psychological terms, that is, the commitment of our all to the person of Jesus. Are we to suppose that it was Christ's intention for there to be two recognized levels of commitment to him? I do not believe so. While the economic expression of commitment may vary, Christ demands everything of his followers. Commitment is meant to be total. What then should the attitude of his followers be to material possessions? How is commitment to be spelled out in terms of lifestyle and economics?

Treasure in heaven

'Do not store up for yourself treasures on earth, where moth and rust destroy, and where thieves break in and steal. But store up for yourselves treasures in heaven, where moth and rust do not destroy, and where thieves do not break in and steal. For where your treasure is, there your heart will be also' (Mt. 6:19–21).

'Do not store up for yourselves treasures on earth.' Is this a command that the followers of Jesus must obey, or is it a recommendation that his followers will do well to adopt? In either case it calls for a radical re-evaluation of our lifestyle. Yet how can we understand the spirit in which our Lord speaks?

Several times in the famous sermon of which these sentences form a part, Jesus contrasted heavenly and earthly perspectives.

'Love your enemies and pray for those who persecute you, *that you may be sons of your Father in heaven.* . . . Be careful not to do your "acts of righteousness" before men, to be seen by them. *If you do, you will have no reward from your Father in heaven. . . .* And when you pray, do not be like the hypocrites, for they love to pray standing in the synagogues and on the street corners to be seen by men. I tell you the truth, they have received their reward in full. But when you pray, go into your room, close the door and pray to your Father, who is unseen. *Then your Father, who sees what is done in secret, will reward you*' (Mt. 5:44–45; 6:1, 5–6; my emphasis).

Repeatedly Jesus shows two radically different ways of viewing things here on earth, the heavenly way and the earthly. If we share one view we will act one way, but if we share the other we will act differently.

Jesus does not seem to exalt poverty. The verse about storing up treasure in heaven is not a command but an appeal to sanctified common sense, or, better, a challenge to the faith of those who profess belief in heavenly realities. Clearly, if earthly treasures are corruptible and insecure, we will do better to employ our time securing heavenly treasure. To transpose the recommendation to the twentieth century, if televisions can go on the blink, cars depreciate, fashionable clothes go out of date, if bonds and jewels can be stolen, insurance companies go bankrupt, banks fail, and war and inflation destroy property and the value of money, it would make more sense to devote our energies to accumulating a celestial fortune.

But notice. Jesus sees earthly and heavenly fortune-hunting to be in competition. ('Do not

store up *A* but store up *B*.') We might prefer it to
be a question of both/and, whereas he seems to
see it as either/or – either treasure on earth or
treasure in heaven. Apparently we cannot hedge
our bets.

But before I follow this idea further, let me be
practical. Is saving wrong? Should we never make
provision for the future? Does the teaching of
Jesus open the way to irresponsibility? Where do
common sense and prudence end and treasure-
hoarding and greed begin? Did our Creator not
teach squirrels to hoard their nuts for winter?

'The diligent man will get precious wealth,'
asserts Solomon (Pr. 12:27, RSV). 'A good man
leaves an inheritance to his children's children'
(Pr. 13:22, RSV). 'The soul of the diligent is richly
supplied' (Pr. 13:4, RSV). We cannot and must not
say that prosperity is any more evil than prudence. Nor may we damn the possession of
wealth.

The problem arises when we start asking how
far we should go either in making provision for
the future or in accumulating things. If Scripture
were to do the decent thing and come right out
with how much hoarding we should do in the
name of responsibility and exactly where the line
lay separating prudence from greed, we would
find it much easier. But Scripture never does and
the Holy Spirit never will. For we are asking the
wrong question. If we read the Sermon on the
Mount carefully, we begin to see that Jesus seems
more concerned with the psychology of the thing.
Having begun by pointing out that it makes better
sense to work for treasures that will last, he
immediately adds enigmatically, 'For where your

treasure is, there your heart will be also'
(Mt. 6:21).

We can infer from his statement that only one
hoard will in practice constitute treasure. Either it
will be the heavenly hoard or it will be the earthly.
It cannot be both. We could almost invert the
words of Jesus and they would still be true.
'Where your heart is, there your treasure will be
also.' Jesus has redefined *treasure* to mean 'that in
which I take my greatest delight and towards
which I devote my greatest efforts'. His interest
seems to lie in what treasure means to us and what
effect it has on us and, particularly, in what it does
to our capacity to see.

'The eye is the lamp of the body. If your eyes
are good, your whole body will be full of light. But
if your eyes are bad, your whole body will be full
of darkness. If then the light within you is darkness, how great is that darkness!' (Mt. 6:22–23).
Having good eyes seems in the context to mean
having a true perspective. So long as we are torn
between material things and heavenly things our
judgment will be clouded, and we will not be
capable of 'seeing' matters as God sees them. On
the other hand, if we are concerned solely with
heavenly treasure and cease to worry about
collecting material things, matters which previously puzzled us will begin to fall into place. But
to be ambivalent is to be confused and uncertain
('full of darkness').

This, too, is a psychological law. Our goal in life
determines our view of life. We see whatever supports the view we already espouse. Conservative
politicians see those things that confirm their position, as do liberals also. We view life through the

tinted spectacles of the philosophy we have already chosen, so that what we see is predetermined by what we are. Butterfield refers to communist and Catholic historians 'screaming across interstellar wastes their respective versions of history', each view reflecting a different mental set.

Since God is at the heart of reality, only by seeking him can we wear untinted glasses and begin to see things as he sees them. Our problem, however, is like that of my Cantonese merchant. We would like to believe that our treasure is in heaven and that heaven is our real choice. But the fact is that we find ourselves filled with anxiety. Earthly treasures continue to attract. We may not want outrageous wealth and would be content with reasonable financial security. But we don't want to miss out on anything either. We are ambivalent. We straddle the fence. Even our goal of 'reasonable financial security' eludes us perpetually, while we try in vain to conjure up a 'treasure' feeling towards heaven. We succeed in neither goal but are, of all men and women, most miserable. We do not possess good eyes and are incapable of willing one thing.

We are like the monkey with its hand trapped inside the coconut shell, clutching a fistful of peanuts. The monkey wants freedom and peanuts, but cannot have both. It must leave the peanuts if it wants to get away. As a matter of fact, it will lose both the peanuts and freedom if it hangs on too long.

And we are caught in a similar bind. We long to be free of earthly entanglements to serve God in the Spirit. Yet we cling to something more elusive than peanuts. We may only want *enough*. But without realizing it, we redefine *enough* again and again with the passage of time. Others of us want to have as much as we can get. So we are full of darkness.

'No one can serve two masters; for either he will hate the one and love the other, or he will be devoted to the one and despise the other. You cannot serve God and mammon' (Mt. 6:24, RSV). *Mammon* refers to money or to material things. Jesus is talking here as though money were a person, a master controlling the lives of his servants. In the ancient world it was inconceivable that a slave, or for that matter a free servant, should serve two masters. Again, the statement is true psychologically as well. In practice I find it impossible to be equally devoted to two major goals. One or the other will become nominal and cease to capture my imagination and my fiercest efforts. We cannot devote our hearts and allegiance equally to God and to mammon.

This terrible principle means that so long as mammon fascinates us God does not number us among those who serve him however much 'Christian work' we do. We were created to have one centre. To try to have two is to be miserable and to enjoy neither spiritual things nor material. It would have been far more pleasant had our consciences never been awakened so as to leave us free to love mammon and mammon alone. As it is we are doomed to dissatisfaction until and unless we slash ourselves free from cords that tie us to mammon or those that bind us to Christ.

The choice for a truly regenerate Christian is a simple one. It lies between the misery of ambivalence and the freedom of valuing Christ, between double darkness and light for the whole body.

If your heart is with the Lord Christ and if you are ardently concerned with the interests of his kingdom, the reasons for the conflict between material possessions and heavenly treasure will become clearer. The more time you devote to meeting with him, worshipping him, learning about him, serving him, the less time you will have available for what is of no value.

The Lord Christ places demands upon his followers which it is their privilege to respond to. His demands differ from those of earthly captains. He insists they let him transform the hours they spend on common tasks – washing, dressing, studying, buying, selling or on working for earthly masters – so that these activities henceforth be performed as acts of worship ardently rendered to his glory. Then he opens new and golden hours that were once vainly wasted so that now they may be devoted to feeding the hungry, clothing the naked, healing the sick, opening the eyes of the blind, comforting the sorrowing and proclaiming his blood-bought liberty for slaves of sin.

Such is the light of glory the Lord Christ sheds on the earthly doings of his followers so that any shoddy rubbish surrounding them is seen for what it is. His followers grow sensitive to the evil of the days they live in and begin to redeem the time. Their focus shifts from a material to a heavenly perspective. Slowly they begin to discover that they scarcely have time to acquire the means to procure their daily needs.

'Do not worry about your life, what you will eat or drink; or about your body, what you will wear,' their Lord tells them. (And with them he tells us also.) 'Is not life more important than food, and the body more important than clothes?' (Mt. 6:25).

When the claims of Christ grip us, we find we have no choice but to trust him about our needs. However great our wealth, we discover that his amazing commands involve walking a pathway of faith. He reminds us of the birds God cares for and of the lilies and the grass. He asks us whether we are not of greater concern to the Father than they, implying that we are absurd to shrink back in fear when the evidence of his providence surrounds us on every hand. 'What will we eat? What will we drink? What will we wear?' he mimics us mockingly, adding scornfully that such panic-filled squeals should come only from the mouths of the godless (Mt. 6:25–32).

He is telling us that God knows we need food and clothing. Presumably he knows about all our other needs. While in this passage Jesus does not promise us riches, he makes it plain that it is absurd that his followers should hang back in doubt and fear.

The basic issue

Jesus finally makes explicit the basic issue he has been talking around all along. 'You of little *faith*,' he calls us (Mt. 6:30). For it is want of faith that makes us opt for earthly rather than heavenly treasure. If we really believed in celestial treasures, who among us would be so stupid as to buy gold? We just do not believe. Heaven is a

154

dream, a religious fantasy which we affirm because we are orthodox. If people believed in heaven, they would spend their time preparing for permanent residence there. But nobody does. We just like the assurance that something nice awaits us *when the real life is over*.

You need only skim superficially over New Testament pages to realize that the focus Jesus has on faith seems to differ from Paul's angle on the same subject. That is not to say that master and follower are in conflict. A moment's thought is enough to see that each has a different question in mind.

'What is it that justifies?' is Paul's question. Faced with false teaching by the circumcision party to the Galatian congregations, false teaching that insisted that Gentile believers be circumcised to fulfill the law of Moses, Paul with two magnificent treatises abolishes from early Christendom any thought that peace with God can be based on anything except faith in Christ. To the question, 'What is it that justifies?' there can be but one answer. 'Faith in Christ justifies – and faith in Christ alone.'

The question Jesus constantly addresses is simpler and more basic. It is, 'Is faith present?' 'When the Son of Man comes,' he once mused, 'will he find faith on the earth?' (Lk. 18:8). He hadn't always found it the first time he came. In his own home town 'he did not do many miracles there because of their lack of faith' (Mt. 13:58). To his humiliated disciples, who asked the reason for their failure to cast a demon out of an epileptic boy, he replied, 'Because you have so little faith' (Mt. 17:20). After he was raised from the

dead, while the same disciples were too dis-
heartened to credit stories of his resurrection, he
appeared to them and reproached them for their
want of faith (Mk. 16:14).

It is not that Jesus failed to teach justification by
faith. While he may not have used the expression,
the concept appears more than once in John's
Gospel (5:24, for example). Nevertheless, the
question that seems to lie behind much of his
teaching remains, 'Where is faith to be found? Is
it present here?' Repeatedly he applauds great
faith and reproves its absence (such as Mt. 6:30;
8:10, 26; 14:31; 16:8; Mk. 4:40; Lk. 7:9; 12:28).

I said that the question 'Is faith present?' is a
simple question, simpler than 'What is it that justifies?' However, we tend to concentrate nowadays
on the Pauline question, almost as if we thought
that by rightly understanding justification by faith
we should automatically possess the faith that justifies. We forget that Melanchthon the scholar
taught that very doctrine to Luther the believer,
but as far as we know Melanchthon, whose
scholarly genius contributed so much to Luther's
Galatian commentary, died an unbeliever. Yet
Luther, who had not really grasped the doctrine
until at least four years after he had completed his
first draft of the Romans commentary (and some
years after he nailed his defiant theses to the door
in Wittenberg), was justified by faith long before
his mind had encompassed the doctrine. It would
appear that one may apprehend and even assent
to the doctrine without possessing the faith the
doctrine speaks of, while another who has not yet
grasped its content may nonetheless have justifying faith.

Jesus' fundamental question remains, then, How can we know when justifying faith is present? How may I know whether it is present in me? Or in western churches? What test can we apply?

One answer Jesus gives is that faith in the invisible God can be demonstrated by power over material things, either power to manipulate them or power to escape enslavement to them. If someone's life is controlled by material things, it is possible that such a person knows nothing of saving faith. One who could not believe something fundamental in the visible universe cannot be expected to believe spiritual reality. Thus of a perplexed Nicodemus Jesus demands, 'I have spoken to you of earthly things and you do not believe; how then will you believe if I speak of heavenly things?' (Jn. 3:12). Again when the scribes criticize the way he pronounces forgiveness of sins over a paralysed man, he asks, 'Which is easier: to say to the paralytic, "Your sins are forgiven," or to say, "Get up, take your mat and walk"?' (Mk. 2:9). He then proceeded to demonstrate his authority in the invisible realm by showing his power over things visible. The paralysed man got up. The scribes were obliged to close their mouths, and all who were present praised God for his power.

Let me restate the principle. We must be suspicious of any faith about personal justification that is not substantiated by faith in God's power over material things in our everyday life. Faith about pie in the sky when I die cannot be demonstrated. Faith that God can supply my need today *can* be demonstrated. And if someone claims to

157

possess justifying faith but shows no evidence of it, we may ask such a person whether he or she understands the difference between faith and mental assent. *Enslavement to the visible makes faith in the invisible suspect.*

What did the young ruler need to do to gain eternal life and heavenly treasure? He needed to sell all he had and to follow Jesus. But he was unable to (Mt. 19:16–22). Why? Because he loved what he trusted, and he trusted his great possessions. He was a slave of the visible. He lacked effective faith in the invisible God. Had he enjoyed such faith, he need not have clung to his riches. He was not damned for possessing them, only for hanging on to them as if they were a lifeboat on a stormy sea.

James also touches the point that clinging to money may indicate the absence of saving faith. 'Suppose a brother or sister is without clothes and daily food. If one of you says to him, "Go, I wish you well; keep warm and well fed," but does nothing about his physical needs, what good is it? In the same way, faith by itself, if it is not accompanied by action, is dead' (Jas. 2:15–17).

The question behind the teaching of Jesus ('Is faith present?') strikes like a dagger into our chests. Do we have faith? Or do our lives consist only in the abundance of our possessions? Are we enslaved by our possessions?

Security. How we plan for it! We save. We invest. We are provident, responsible. We think of our old age and of our children's educations. Little by little we build our tiny fortresses, hiding from the threat of penury behind savings, locks and bolts. Inflation? Some of us may be worried enough to invest in things we hope inflation will not affect. Others among us smile secretly, for we are experienced investors and feel we have solved the problem.

We are like the rich fool. Our professions and businesses have brought forth plentifully. We have more money than we need – even after giving our tithes. What can we do? We discuss matters carefully with our accountants, and having acted on sound advice we tell ourselves, 'We now have ample reserves. Let us travel abroad in winter and spend our summers with the children. We have earned it. It's time we took things easy!'

The rich fool (Lk. 12:15–21) was not a fool for harvesting abundant crops. He was a fool for letting his crops fill his horizon and determine his lifestyle. He was a slave to barns and grain, and seems to have had no interest in God. When God's awful voice awakened him from his dreams saying, 'You fool! This very night your life will be demanded from you. Then who will get what you have prepared for yourself?' he had to leave his barns and enter the Presence naked. Had he sent anything on in advance? Jesus didn't say. Presumably he had forwarded nothing. His heart was back among his mountains of grain.

But notice the conclusions we have reached. The thrust of Jesus' teaching does not deal with the virtues of poverty or the sin of riches. Rather, he seeks to show us first the greater value of heavenly treasure and the folly of seeking earthly. Then he warns us of the seductive power of riches, the love of which draws our hearts away from him and renders us incapable of serving him. Finally he upbraids us with the unbelief which underlies our anxiety about our material needs.

The good of creation

The desire to possess material things and a love of the things of God are in conflict. This might lead us to suppose that material things are bad and heavenly things good. Is this really so?

Christianity has from time to time been adulterated by teachings wholly alien to it. From its earliest days it was plagued by gnosticism and by a dualistic view of human nature and the cosmos. Spirit was what mattered. Our bodies were either essentially evil or else unimportant.

This idea has many forms and still exists under different guises among professing Christians. I suppose we could accuse the gnostics of being the polar opposites of pragmatic materialists.

Instead of declaring that matter is all that matters, some might say that spirit is all that matters. Such a view calls for a downplaying of the physical creation. Riches, houses, food, sex, forests, mountains, flowers and whatever you like to name are at best irrelevant and at worst evil. Therefore the good consists in a divorce of matter from spirit. This means that either I need not concern myself with what my body does (allowing it to indulge itself in any excess, for sin also becomes unimportant) or I deny it any physical gratification in the interests of my spiritual and intellectual development. Thus asceticism is a country cousin of gnosticism.

Jesus taught us to despise neither our bodies nor material things. There is virtue neither in carelessly indulging our bodies nor in subjecting them to ritual neglect. So Paul in his Colossian letter writes,

> Since you died wth Christ to the basic principles of this world, why, as though you still belonged to it, do you submit to its rules: 'Do not handle! Do not taste! Do not touch!' These are all destined to perish with use, because they are based on human commands and teachings. Such regulations indeed have an appearance of wisdom, with their self-imposed worship, their false humility and their harsh treatment of the body, but they lack any value in restraining sensual indulgence (Col. 2:20–23).

The physical universe was created by God. He pronounced it good (Gn. 1:31). Even though it is now tainted by sin, it still reflects his majesty, his beauty, his glory. Matter is not evil, it is only that we have made an evil use of it, becoming idolatrous in our attitude to it, chaining ourselves with gold chains. We have made the good the enemy of the best. We have worshipped the creature rather than the Creator.

Because matter is good, God may reward those he loves with an abundance of it. 'After Job had prayed for his friends, the LORD made him prosperous again and gave him twice as much as he had before' (Jb. 42:10).

Jesus mentioned precisely such a reward in the Sermon on the Mount. 'But seek first [God's] kingdom and his righteousness, and all these things will be given to you as well' (Mt. 6:33). The phrase 'all these things' refers to food and clothing. We might call them necessities rather than rewards. The point is that whatever we call them, they are given by the heavenly Father, and therefore must be good things, since he does not give his children evil gifts (Mt. 7:11). Paul makes matters explicit in his first letter to Timothy when, probably referring to some gnostics, he says that they 'forbid people to marry and order them to abstain from certain foods, which God created to be received with thanksgiving by those who believe and who know the truth. For everything God created is good, and nothing is to be rejected if it is received with thanksgiving' (1 Tim. 4:3–4).

We must not combat materialism by embracing the opposite error of asceticism. There is no virtue in poverty unless in the course of our obedience to God we have to endure poverty because of a greater end. Many missionaries endure relative poverty – relative, that is, to what they might have enjoyed (though not relative to the people they minister to) had they not opted to serve God in foreign missions. Poverty in that case is an occupational hazard. Wise missionaries accept relative poverty in order not to raise unnecessary barriers between themselves and the people they serve. These missionaries do not exactly embrace poverty. They are (or should be) indifferent to it, content to be poor if being poor facilitates the work being carried out.

Jesus accepted poverty not because it was virtuous but because to save us he had to leave heaven's riches and become human. Paul points to Christ's poverty when he exhorts the Corinthian church to give to relief work. 'For you know the grace of our Lord Jesus Christ, that though he was rich, yet for your sakes he became poor, so that you through his poverty might become rich' (2 Cor. 8:9).

We are called not to imitate Christ's poverty but to follow him in his example of love and self-giving, not caring whether we be poor or rich so long as we follow him and do his will. Should he heap material riches upon us, well and good. But if our lot should be one of pain and penury, we are to laugh at our difficulties, counting them as nothing, 'looking to Jesus, the pioneer and perfecter of our faith, who for the joy that was set before him endured the cross, despising the shame' (Heb. 12:2, RSV). He had contempt for what he underwent. We too, should hardship come upon us, are called to despise it, thinking only of the glory of our task and of our Leader.

The peril of wealth

Abundance may or may not represent God's goodness to a man or woman. It may merely indicate industry or the good fortune to inherit riches or that the rich person is a crook. We must never assume that to be wealthy is *ipso facto* to be in God's good books. There are extremely wicked rich people just as there are godly rich.

A careful reading of the Bible indicates that the rich are condemned only for the misuse of riches. I mentioned earlier that Christ's concern about material possessions had to do with the effect they have on our relationship with him and on our relationships with our neighbours. Both are present in his recommendation for the rich young ruler. He was to sell all he had in order to give to

163

the poor (that is, to be concerned with his needy neighbour) and to follow Christ (Mt. 19:16–22).

The two relationships go hand in hand. They cannot be separated; concern for one's neighbour arises out of a true relationship with God. When asked to cite 'the great commandment,' Jesus immediately quoted two. '"Love the Lord your God with all your heart and with all your soul and with all your mind." This is the first and greatest commandment. And the second is like it: "Love your neighbour as yourself." All the Law and the Prophets hang on these two commandments' (Mt. 22:37–40). Given that upon these two loves (of God and of one's neighbour) hang all biblical teaching about our duty, it makes sense that God's concern about wealth should focus on how it affects our relationship with him and how it affects our relationship with our neighbour.

These concerns are present in the Old Testament as well as the New. It is sometimes suggested that Amos, to take one example, damned riches in themselves. But this is not so.

> For three sins of Israel,
> even for four, I will not turn back my wrath.
> They sell the righteous for silver,
> and the needy for a pair of sandals.
> They trample on the heads of the poor
> as upon the dust of the ground
> and deny justice to the oppressed.
>
> (Am. 2:6–7)

He speaks of Samaria's rich women as those 'who oppress the poor and crush the needy' (Am. 4:1). The Samaritan rich were exploiters of the poor, and it was against their heartless oppression that the prophet spoke.

Concern for the poor neighbour is evident in the primitive church. Clarifying his relationship with the apostles in Jerusalem, Paul remarks, 'All they asked was that we should continue to remember the poor, the very thing I was eager to do' (Gal. 2:10). Paul condemned bad conduct around the Lord's Table in Corinth not primarily because of the drunkenness of the richer members but because of their heartless snobbery. The rich brought food and wine for their social peers, thus cutting themselves off from their poorer brothers and sisters and causing division in Christ's body.

> When you come together, it is not the Lord's Supper you eat, for as you eat, each of you goes ahead without waiting for anybody else. One remains hungry, another gets drunk. Don't you have homes to eat and drink in? Or do you despise the church of God and humiliate those who have nothing? What shall I say to you? Shall I praise you for this? Certainly not! (1 Cor. 11:20–22).

'Now listen, you rich people,' writes James, 'weep and wail because of the misery that is coming upon you. Your wealth has rotted, and moths have eaten your clothes. Your gold and silver are corroded. Their corrosion will testify against you and eat your flesh like fire' (Jas. 5:1–3). James speaks prophetically. He looks into the future and sees the terrible judgment that will come upon rich people. But again, is it of being rich that James accuses them? No. He continues,

> Look! The wages you failed to pay the workmen who mowed your fields are crying out against you. The cries of the harvesters have reached the ears of the Lord Almighty. You have lived on earth in luxury and self-indulgence. You have fattened yourselves in the day of slaughter. You have condemned and murdered innocent men, who were not opposing you (Jas. 5:4–6).

The wealthy wallowed in the luxury of riches they had acquired by paying low wages, by callous indifference to the poor and by flagrant injustice. They could kill and extort because they had power.

Riches are not evil but they are dangerous. Happy are those who are not beguiled by them, for such people are few! 'I tell you the truth, it is hard for a rich man to enter the kingdom of heaven. Again I tell you, it is easier for a camel to go through the eye of a needle than for a rich man to enter the kingdom of God' (Mt. 19:23–24).

Riches corrupt everybody who is in the least corruptible. God is merciful and can deliver the rich from the danger of being rich. But many of us do not want to be delivered. We say we trust God. But we act as though our trust were in riches, as indeed it often is. Riches undermine faith.

We live in a day when those in business (not all of whom are rich) who claim to be born again have facilitated their business relationships by publishing evangelical yellow pages. We could argue about the rights and wrongs of such listings, but what troubles me is to see the name of Christ publicly linked with some businesses that seem to be highly unethical, even though their owners or directors profess to know Christ.

My wife and I prefer to avoid doing business with Christians unless they are personally known to us as trustworthy. Two things concern us. First, we do not want to join the crowd of people who go to such Christians under the impression that by claiming to belong to Christ they can expect a better deal than non-Christians would get. Second, we have also found from experience that someone in business who professes Christianity is just as likely to give us a dishonest deal as a non-Christian is. Unjust trading and exploitation of employees seem to go together. In saying this I must make it clear that I know Christians in business who excel both in their competence and their integrity and who clearly have not sold out to mammon. But there are others who exploit employees and customers alike, and I am filled with shame when I think of them. It is of such that James speaks.

We must leave their judgment to God and possess our souls in patience. We are in no position to condemn people richer than ourselves if we have not known the terrible power of possessions. 'Give me neither poverty nor riches,' pleaded Agur the son of Jakeh, 'but give me only my daily bread. Otherwise, I may have too much and disown you and say, "Who is the LORD?" Or I may become poor and steal' (Pr. 30:8–9).

Corporate riches

Riches do not only affect us in our personal affairs. They equally affect us in our corporate relationships. Some clubs are snobbish and boast luxurious facilities, pandering to the egos of their members. Beautiful, ornate buildings and facilities do the same. Those of us who do not possess personal riches may gain vicarious satisfaction by belonging to such clubs.

There is a threat that riches will corrupt our personal and corporate affairs in church too. We may become spiritual snobs, wanting fellowship only with 'the right kind' of Christian people, unconsciously excluding racial minorities or the uneducated, and certainly those who are down-and-out. Not only does corporate wealth affect our relations with others, it undermines our faith in God as well as our dependence upon the Holy Spirit. It only makes sense that its effects on our personal lives will be no different from our corporate life.

If the majority of church members and the members of the governing body have never in their own lives resolved the issue of treasure in heaven, is it not inevitable that their uncertainty will be expressed in the church's policies and outlook? By this I do not mean that the church will cease to proclaim the gospel or to value Scripture. You can preach the gospel for many reasons. You may do so to glorify Christ and because you share his concern for lost sheep. Or you may simply want to swell the congregation, to make your church a winner in the competition of growing congregations.

What springs first into your mind when you think of your local church? Its buildings and facilities? The pastor? The Sunday-morning turnout? The choir? The Sunday school? Or do you think of a body of people with needs and longings?

Where would the earthly Jesus fit into its congregational organization? Do those who control the plant and finances reflect the otherworldly outlook of the apostles? Do members of the congregation concern themselves more with heavenly treasure than with earthly prestige and comfort? Is the pastor concerned more with a building programme than with making disciples?

What about you? Let me level with you. I have never found mammon easy to get away from. While I renounced my allegiance to him many years ago, he continually sends his emissaries to tempt me. My ears are often deafened by the noise of his propaganda while my eyes swim with the attractive pictures he paints. When it comes to the crunch I know which side I'm on, and I try to make a right decision, but I cannot say the decision is always painless. At times I have to opt for heavenly treasure in the teeth of my yearning to possess. But I am grateful that I experience increasing liberty as I choose Christ.

There may be no point in your reading further in this book unless you have given serious thought to your personal priorities. The book assumes that material things corrupt. Unless you are so convinced of this that you opt for heaven, whatever the decision may cost you, then your concern for the church's materialism will not lead to change.

I cannot quote admonitions to rich churches in the New Testament, since there do not seem to have been any rich churches. Paul told the Corinthian Christians, who seemed to think highly of themselves, 'Brothers, think of what you were when you were called. Not many of you were wise by human standards; not many were influential; not many were of noble birth. But God chose the foolish things of the world . . . the weak things . . . the lowly things' (1 Cor. 1:26–28.) The Corinthians may not have had material riches to count on, but they seemed to be worldly rather than heavenly in their outlook.

The first hint of corporate riches comes in our Lord's epistle to the loathsomely lukewarm church at Laodicea. 'You say, "I am rich; I have acquired wealth and do not need a thing." But you do not realize that you are wretched, pitiful, poor, blind and naked' (Rev. 3:17). Material riches had cooled their ardour as it cools the spiritual ardour of many a modern congregation.

The most terrifying effect of Christian corporate riches is that faith in God is substituted by business know-how and dependence on technical methodology.

Many years ago I stood one night in the rain, looking wonderingly at the walls of what was then the China Inland Mission headquarters in London. I had read many CIM books, including the two-volume biography of Hudson Taylor, and had been thrilled and quickened by the way God had supplied the mission's needs 'through prayer to God alone' (which I discussed in chapter four).

That night as I looked at the dirty but solid brick wall, I reached out my hand to touch it. It seemed like a holy thing. Not that the CIM was anything other than a human organization blessed and used by God. But to me the walls were an awesome and tangible monument to the reality of God's response to faith. It was as though God himself had put them there. 'This is what God did,' I said, glowing warmly, feeling the solidity of the wet bricks as awe stole over my whole body. 'A solid monument to God's response to faith.'

There are many so-called monuments to faith around the world today. People would like us to believe that God raised them in answer to believing prayer. I don't think so. Many are monuments to human ingenuity, to public relations know-how, to clever advertising, to skill in milking Christian suckers. And since we would not need to depend on public relations know-how and clever advertising if we truly believed in God, I suppose it is correct to say that the buildings of which I speak are monuments to unbelief rather than monuments to faith. We view them with understandable (but culpable) pride. We have made it. We need nothing.

May God have mercy on us! For we are wretched, pitiful, poor, blind and naked.

171

Chapter Twelve

The golden cow

In his role as the last and greatest prophet, Jesus warned his followers about forgetting to whom they belonged and selling themselves to mammon. Against commercialized desecration of the temple he acted violently, expressing the same moral reprehension that inspired earlier prophets to call God's people a whore.

The twentieth-century church has also forgotten which master she belongs to, painting herself like a hussy in her silly pursuit of Lord Mammon. Or, to use another image, the church has gone a-whoring after a golden cow.

Not a calf, if you please, but a cow. I call her a *golden* cow because her udders are engorged with liquid gold, especially in the West, where she grazes in meadows lush with greenbacks. Her priests placate her by slaughtering godly principles, upon whose blood she looks with tranquil satisfaction.

Anxious rows of worshippers bow down before their buckets. Although the gold squirts endlessly, the worshippers are trembling lest the supply of sacrificial victims should one day fail to appease her.

I used to be angry with my fellow fundamentalists and outraged at certain evangelical institutions because of their materialistic attitudes. But my rage has long since subsided. I even went through a charitable and patronizing stage. May God forgive me. Who am I to rage or to patronize?

I know some children whose mothers are whores. Can you imagine what it feels like to discover your mother goes to bed with men for money? In point of fact such children feel a variety of emotions, ranging from indifference to bitter rejection to shame to (occasionally) hurt mingled with compassion. It's hard to quit loving your own mother, even if she is a whore. You've only got one.

Fundamentalism is my mother. I was nurtured in her warm bosom. She cared for me with love and taught me all she knew. I owe her (humanly speaking) my life, my spiritual food and many of my early joys. She introduced me to the Saviour and taught me to feed on the bread of life. Our relationship wasn't all honey and roses, but she was the only mother I had. I clung to her then and find it hard not to lean on her now. If she let me down at times, I'm old enough to realize that no mother is perfect. But to find out that she was a whore, that she let herself be used by mammon, was another matter. And as the wider evangelical movement gradually took her place in my life, it was painful to make the same discovery twice.

Yet we are still family. I am still a part of the evangelical movement. We are, as it were, of the same flesh and blood.

Collective responsibility

In the last chapter I referred to the way riches affect us corporately. We bear a collective responsibility for the worship I refer to, even though as individuals some of us may believe we worship only the one true God. There were many prophets who had not bowed the knee to Baal in Elijah's day, yet all Israel suffered the seven-year drought.

Wide differences in practice and in attitudes characterize different Christians, so that when I make a generalization it may seem unfair. Yet in ways God holds us, I believe, collectively responsible for what goes on among us. We draw away from one another into distinct groups and church organizations, indulging in the liberty this gives us to criticize another group as though we ourselves had no connection with it. We are obsessed by the individualism of the culture we live in. Yet in Christ we are one body. Shall one eye say to the other, 'Poor toe, it's got cancer'? When I make a generalization, then, I make it with the full awareness of the wide differences that exist and with the hope that we will not all delight in a false liberty to point fingers while remaining immune from guilt ourselves.

Let me expand, too, on what I mean by worshipping the golden cow. Is mass advertising wrong? Is it wrong for Christian groups to be concerned with their relations with the public?

174

Without giving the matter much thought I would answer no to both questions, but the questions themselves are naive.

No, when I talk about worshipping the golden cow, I am talking about a particular form of materialism to which we have fallen prey. It is a way of life that sets our feet on the road to spiritual harlotry. And I think it will be better for me to describe the materialistic way of life I refer to rather than define it. I may succeed in showing how and why we have become materialists and that we bear more than a collective guilt. For while it is true that Christian institutions follow such ritual forms of worship as mass advertising and public relations techniques, they would never do so if the rest of us were not also guilty at heart of a greed for things.

Priests of the new worship

If you were to ask what kind of person typifies the twentieth century, I think many people's minds would flash to astronauts. Yet the person who expresses the spirit of our age more than any other is not the astronaut but the salesperson.

Most of us live lives far removed from space platforms. We spend our days earning money to pay for the cars we bought and our evenings and weekends spending more money, the money we hope to earn tomorrow. Our grasping arms are being crammed with the produce of an age of abundance, our eagerness to grasp being more than matched by the zeal of the people who would shower such produce upon us. Abundance in the West has become a menace, threatening to inundate us under mountains of television sets, houses, clothes, flowery toilet paper, cars, books, furniture, computers and gadgets of every kind. To avoid being deluged, we must keep the goods moving. Advertising has been carried to lengths never before known. Our letterboxes, telephones, radios and televisions are channels for would-be sellers of merchandise, who are hard put to get rid of what the manufacturers produce.

There is nothing wrong, of course, with a proper distribution of goods and services. I am not talking about that but about the promotion of superabundance. We need food, clothing and shelter. Even abundance and comfort are gifts of God. But we are no longer his creatures accepting and distributing the goodness he pours upon us but the feverish and slavish worshippers of abundance itself.

So the sound of your doorbell may herald the double-glazing salesman or the Avon lady. The ring of the telephone may precede slick patter from a bogus researcher or an invitation to a party where anything from clothes and coffee to toys and tea lends an air of friendly neighbourhood fun to the deadly business of keeping the economy expanding. If we leave our homes, we still cannot escape, for our eyes are assailed by billboards and our ears by commercials on the car radio. (It sometimes amuses me to speculate that the most prized art of an age to come may be a twentieth-century television commercial.)

The life force of the vast and complex sales organization is an army of sales representatives, varying widely in background, training and ethical standards. Some are college graduates; others never finished grade school. Some fly first class and enter into delicate negotiations with city halls and directors of companies. Others trudge from door to door in suburbia or sit with telephone books in their lap dialling numbers. Some are conscientious and have high ethical standards. Others are grubby con men. Yet their goal is a common one: to sell you and me as much of their company's produce as they can. They are the priests of the god of greed.

When you ask sales reps how they view their method of earning a living, they may tell you that they are carrying out a public service. Their function is to find what your need is and to meet it. It is not in their interest or yours (they will say) to foist on you a product you neither need nor want. And in performing a service for you, they are not only helping you by providing a product but helping themselves by gaining a commission. The more their company can profit from sales, the greater will be its growth and therefore its ability to bring prosperity to the whole community. (And prosperity, remember, means more abundance all around.) By competing with sales of inferior articles, they are also helping to improve standards. Inferior articles become extinct monsters in a sort of survival of the commercially fittest.

All of us recognize that bad salespeople – bad in the moral sense – exist. But equally we recognize that there are good ones, good in the sense that they do not allow their urge to clinch a sale to override their sense of fairness to the customer. Chambers of commerce as well as organizations such as the Christian Businessmen's Committee exist among other things to promote more ethical business practices (though how successful they are in doing so is cast in doubt by the growth of consumer organizations).

But what of the system of which salespeople are so vitally a part? If we shift our perspective for a moment, we shall see that far from being the central character in the twentieth-century drama, the sales representative in turn is but a puppet manipulated by more powerful hands. Indeed, we may see more still. We shall see, if we look hard enough, that the system could not operate apart from human greed, the greed all of us share.

Does modern advertising really help manufacturers meet society's need by making us all aware of how and where our needs can be met? Or do advertising and sales people, in the complex sales structure of which they form a part, trade on our greed by creating artificial needs so as to market unneeded products? They probably do both, but their real prosperity lies in doing the latter.

The cow is a cheat

Social critics have for some years been decrying advertisers. Many have attacked the forced obsolescence that is the basis of many western economies. Disturbing questions are being asked.

How does one define *need* in a society where standards of living are constantly rising? Is microwave popcorn *necessary* in any sense of the word? What is to be said of our sense of values when millions of dollars were invested in making and marketing it at a time when people in India were concerned with keeping themselves and their children from starvation? How *necessary* is flowered underwear for men, or any other change of fashion in cars, houses, clothes or bath-room fittings? How about the 'need' for shifting hemlines up or down? Or frozen dinners?

Again, how do the generals of the sales army in their carpeted offices plot their strategy for meeting our 'needs'? What angles do they play on besides our greed? Our anxieties? (Is your family protected?) Our sexual preoccupations? (Does your breath rob you of kisses?) Our guilt? Our snobbery? (You deserve the best.)

Is it right that society gain prosperity from cigarette sales at the cost of people gasping and coughing with lung cancer? Or from alcohol commercials when others die of liver failure? How do we view a system that is upheld, at least in part, by a calculated appeal to our psychological weaknesses?

And having asked such critical questions about mass advertising, what are we saying about ourselves, especially about ourselves as Christians? What kind of blind fools are we to be duped by the worship of the god of greed? Do we really believe his promises to give us happiness? And if we say we don't, why do we pour out our money in offerings to him? If you think a little more about it you will begin to see that the sales people, the advertisers and all of us who fall for their ploys are deceived victims of the same god who will ultimately destroy us all.

Take sales reps again. How fair is the system to them? What about the rosy pictures painted for them at sales conventions? Is it fair to 'psych up' people who never could and never will make their fortune (or even their living) in selling, so as to squeeze a few more ounces out of their mediocre potential? It may benefit the company and perhaps the economy too, but what about those who in middle age are slowly beginning to realize that the beautiful mirage that fired their enthusiasm is the creation of false prophets of a commercial religion? Are sales reps priests of a false religion, or are they donkeys led on by dangling carrots?

Some years ago Arthur Miller wrote a play entitled *Death of a Salesman*. Willy Loman (the salesman) is movingly portrayed in middle age as a bewildered and pathetic man struggling against odds to preserve the dream of a life that was to be. Because of urban development, his home 'in the country' is, by the time he has paid for it, dwarfed by high-rise apartments. It is impossible to view him in any other way than as a victim. His suicide and the questions it raises for all of us are more than good drama. Throughout Europe, the western hemisphere, East Asia – indeed, everywhere except perhaps in some of the few remaining communist countries – thousands of Willy Lomans set out with shining eyes, only to encounter eventual disenchantment, alcoholism or the acceptance of living a life of failure.

The god of greed is a cheat. His promise of material rewards may never even be kept. He cheats his priests as much as he cheats his worshippers, turning his back on both and leaving them to their despair once he no longer has use for them. And even those upon whom he lavishes his rewards find them strangely flat. His flowers are made of plastic and his food of sawdust, while his wine can neither refresh nor intoxicate. His delights have the power to dazzle and excite, but they can satisfy nobody.

I hope I have made it clear that in labelling salespeople and advertising copywriters as priests and prophets of the golden cow I am not singling them out as the heart of the evil system. They may exemplify it, or even symbolize it, but they are not in any sense the key to it. Unless you grasp this you will mistake my writing for a sociological treatise knocking big business and the free-enterprise system. It is too easy to present the capitalists, the bankers, the industrial tycoons as the villains of the piece, even though there may be some justice in doing so. Yet if they (as many people tell us) exploit us, do we not make their task all the easier because we are selfish and greedy?

And how do we regard the growth of consumer organizations? Righteousness is on their side, you tell me, but I will answer that greed is in the hearts of their founders also. Their cause, and I will concede the point, is a just one. The prophets themselves denounced wealthy oppressors of the poor. Yet I cannot escape the feeling that all of us – producers, consumers, employers, employees, industrialists, trade unions and advertisers – are tarred with the same brush. I get exactly the same acquisitive feelings rising in me whether I read financial newspapers or consumer magazines.

Sponges soaked with society's values

What does it all boil down to? It comes to this: we Christians are too often like sponges soaked to capacity with the value system of the society we live in. Whether we sympathize with labour or industry, whether we are conservatives, liberals, socialists or whatever, our value systems in practice are one. We may argue fiercely with one another, but we base our arguments on the same premise: the greatest good in life is a bigger (or better-cooked) slice of this world's pie, a pie to which we all have an inalienable right.

And it is precisely here, in our unconscious acceptance of a false value system (with its confusion about our 'rights') that the root of the problem lies. Here lies the weakness that makes us prone to spiritual harlotry. For we have over-valued material prosperity and have under-estimated, taken for granted or even forgotten the God of power and love we profess to worship. We claim to have faith in him. But so long as we are harassed by anxiety about our financial security or overly impressed by the importance of money in Christian work, our profession is hollow and our footsteps follow the pathway to whoredom.

I can claim no immunity to such wrong values. I am myself the kind of sucker who avidly reads a get-rich-quick book. I anxiously weigh the pros and cons of pension schemes versus investment in property as hedges against inflation. And why? It is because I, too, breathe the air full of the incense offered to the cow. So far as I (the carnal I) am concerned, the Sermon on the Mount can cheerfully be relegated to the kingdom age. I am by no means sure that it is safe to take no anxious thought for tomorrow. What guarantee is there that seeking first the kingdom of God and his righteousness will mean that 'all these things' will be added unto me? Is there no fine print under the guarantee?

But here I blame the churches. Where are the preachers who expound to me these Scriptures? Dispensationalists and non-dispensationalists can agree or disagree on the hermeneutics of Matthew 6. But I believe the real reason we avoid such passages or hedge them with words like *but, mind you, on the other hand* and *we must always bear in mind* has nothing to do with dispensational theology. It is due to our secret worship of the cow.

Let the preachers remind the church again that no-one can serve two masters! Never mind the congregation members who get sore and defensive. Let us tell men and women that *you cannot serve God and mammon* even in the church age.

Let us hammer the message home in churches all over the West. Let us raise from the pulpit the practical issues in our own cities, the neighbourhoods of our own churches. City hall will never solve the problems of the inner-city poor. Political skullduggery and the abuse of welfare do not excuse us from finding those to whom we can become neighbours. Let us appoint church committees composed of Christian welfare workers, social workers and journalists to assess the needs in our own areas and to make specific recommendations by which we (without city hall) may take the lead in promoting social reform.

At least a part of the church is being made in the image of western materialism. The tragic outcome of this is a movement which often uses the preaching of the gospel as a means of organizational self-aggrandizement. A few knees have not bowed down before the golden cow, but they are growing fewer. I am writing with the hope that my words will encourage the few who are left and persuade the many who are wavering between God and green dollars while there is time – time which (as the next chapter suggests) may be shorter than we suspect.

Part three: God's judgment and our repentance

Chapter Thirteen

The lashes of divine judgment

Does God's judgment await us for our sins of greed? In chapter one we saw that the Lord of the church judges both Christians and evildoers. Whether, for example, you insist that Revelation 2 – 3 is addressed to real first-century churches or that here Jesus addresses future church ages, it is all one. Christ pronounces judgment on his people.

In the book of Revelation he makes several different threats. 'If you do not repent, I will come to you and remove your lampstand from its place' (2:5). 'I will soon come to you and will fight against them with the sword of my mouth' (2:16). 'I will cast her on a bed of suffering, and I will make those who commit adultery with her suffer intensely, unless they repent of her ways. I will strike her children dead' (2:22–23). 'I am about to spit you out of my mouth' (3:16).

We could say the judgments were of two sorts – spiritual and physical. 'I will remove your lampstand.' (I will remove my holy presence from your midst. You will have no power, no warmth, no true light, no life. You will become a dead, empty shell of a church, a building where people congregate, a purely human activity bereft of any touch of heaven.) 'I will fight against them with the sword of my mouth.' (God's Word will cut down the unrepentant with shattering power. The hammer will break the rock in pieces.) While the imagery John uses is physical, the judgments described here are spiritual. One of them is negative (the removal of spiritual presence); the other is positive (the terrifying power of the convicting Word). But physical judgments are spoken of too – sickness, tribulation, death.

How are we to understand them? We can conceive physical judgments on the nation of Israel. Foreign armies overran her, raped her, took her people into captivity. But how can we conceive of foreign armies in relation to the church? And if physical persecution falls on the church, how may we distinguish between divine judgment and Satanic opposition? When rioters burn down a church building or when secret police seize Christian leaders in the cold hours before dawn, how do we interpret what is happening?

Clearly both kinds of trouble await us. There will be divine judgments executed against a harlot church unless she repents, and they may sometimes take a physical form. There will also be Satan-inspired persecution against the faithful. Infidelity will be rewarded with judgment, faithfulness with persecution. We may make our grim choice.

But if we are to talk of judgment, we must remember something else. Judgment is on-going as well as ultimate. It proceeds throughout history as well as in one final winding-up. We must also remember that God judges sin in nations as well as in churches, and while he will clearly differentiate in his expectations and in his reaction to each, the means by which judgment will descend on both need not differ.

If we take what has happened under right-wing and left-wing tyranny during the past century, we may begin to see how it all works out in practice. Tyranny overcomes a people. At times both people and church are affected, though perhaps in different ways. Churches may be asked by tyrannical governments (for example, in China, in Cuba, in Nazi Germany, in right-wing Chile) to collaborate with the government in maintaining order. The appeal seems innocent enough, even scriptural. It involves organizations or religious bodies in such a way that an authority structure can extend from government to the local congregation.

But slowly its evils become apparent. A church may be expected to extol a political leader. I remember the tears and sighs of a Christian student years ago who described church life under Trujillo in what is now the Dominican Republic. 'My father was an elder in our assembly and a member of the secret police,' he told me. 'His spiritual life was virtually nil. His influence in the church was exercised mainly through me. On Trujillo Day I was expected to speak at several

189

churches on the virtues of Trujillo. I knew what the secret police were doing. Some of my friends had been tortured. Yet if I refused to preach the praises of Trujillo, not only was my dad in trouble, but there would be reprisals against the church. My mother would come and weep before me until I consented to do it.'

It is a common story, and I could multiply examples of the subtle and complex situations arising. They are not few. Nero worship was a problem facing the church in the first century.

What happens under such an oppressive regime is that the church slowly moves into a position of compromise over spiritual issues (that is to say, over who is Lord, Jesus or the current head of state). If it fails to do so it is obliged to accept all the consequences of being secretly 'uncooperative'. The church that compromises, that accepts alliance with the state, is stripped like the harlot she is and shamed. She is stripped of all real authority. The government smiles scornfully at her leaders. The head of the secret police has them all in his pocket. Everyone, people and government alike, know what the real score is. She is stripped of honour, stripped of pride, stripped of glory, stripped sometimes of property and assigned inferior places to meet in. Her autonomy is gone. She is the slave and tool of the state.

It would seem that the most terrible judgments of God toward the church are not physical but spiritual. The candlestick is removed. The harlot is made bare. She is exposed in her shame for all to see.

God's physical judgments seem on the other hand to be exercised against individuals or parties *within* a living church and are designed to cut out a cancer, leaving the church bleeding but ready to be healed. There should be no problem in distinguishing between Satanic opposition and divine judgment. What we may underestimate is the shame, depression and empty futility of the life of the church that has become a collaborator of the modern state.

We are in fact already making ourselves vulnerable to such a fate. Not only have we accepted western values, becoming worshippers of the golden cow, turning ourselves from churches into Christian business enterprises, Christian industries and Christian social clubs, but we have made it clear that to be a good Christian is to be a good American, a good Canadian, a good Briton or whatever. The distinction between citizenship of heaven and earthly citizenship is becoming blurred.

Jeremiah, whose loyalty to Judah never faltered (for he never ceased to serve Judah's true interests), wound up being regarded as a traitor to his country. Few modern Christians are in any such danger. We accept all too naively the essential rightness of the country we live in. And pain, terrible pain, awaits us. Years of aching and longing. Years of emptiness and meaninglessness. Happy are they who are tortured and go to jail, for they shall know the glory of the Lord! Woe to those who bow to Nero, for they shall hunger and lack bread; they shall thirst and have no drink, shiver and remain naked to winds of the North.

It is frightful to consider what it might be like for God's judgment to fall upon us. But we must face this issue squarely. In Romans 1, Paul gives the clearest exposition of the stages of God's judgment. Let us examine them, one lash at a time.

Lash 1: We become blind idiots

One cannot turn from truth without becoming subject to the power of the lie. A 'judicial blindness' falls on all who reject God's presence and rule among us. It is both a self-imposed and a God-imposed blindness. God's judgment begins with *giving us over to the folly we have chosen.* 'For although they knew God, they neither glorified him as God nor gave thanks to him, *but their thinking became futile and their foolish hearts were darkened. Although they claimed to be wise, they became fools*' (Rom. 1:21–22). The sin? Not honouring God as holy, not having a posture of profound gratitude.

Such sin is always associated with pride. We might label it self-sufficiency, but it amounts to the same thing. Either we depend on, glorify, fear, honour and love God, or we transfer those same attitudes to ourselves. and pride blinds us to sin's true nature.

If we trace the roots of every sin deep into the soil of our souls, we find, sooner or later, that we are dealing with self-sufficiency and pride. For instance, greed springs from pride. When God is truly our sufficiency we have everything we could ever want. When he is not our sufficiency, we want something else to take his place. It follows that pride spawns materialism, a greed for things. From pride also springs every kind of lust, since lust is essentially greed. Anger and hate become possible through pride. Why? Pride places us in competition with our fellows; our needs and ambitions compete with theirs. When they beat us

192

in competition we see them as having taken that which is ours. So we hate them. And so we could continue.

What matters is that, being blinded by pride to the real nature of these sins, we fail to see them in their true colours. We can then deny that God really is all-in-all and that life based on any other premises leads to death.

Believe a lie and you are subject to further deception. 'I can handle alcohol,' says the drunkard, too proud to admit his weakness. He buys the lie and continues to drink excessively. He both has been given over and has given himself over to darkness and folly. A dark cloud obscures his understanding. 'I'm still okay to drive,' he says as he continues to drink and proceeds to kill himself and others with him. Pride blinds and blindness is deadly.

I can think of nothing more frightening than intellectual and spiritual blindness. Frequently I beg God to show me my sin. The thought that I might have closed my ears to his voice or my eyes to the true nature of my actions fills me with dread. Many Christians are blind. Look at your friends' lives if you don't believe me. You might feel you're the only one among them who sees things clearly.

Radio, television and news magazines fling lies in our faces all day, every day. Our educational system is a confusing mixture of lies and truth. Democratic governments are not known for strict veracity. After all, the father of lies still rules here, defeated or not. Like Hitler after the Normandy landings, Satan is defeated, *but fights on.*[1]

Believe a small lie and your mind is darkened a little. Believe a big lie and you are really in trouble.

What matters is not the lie itself but our reason for believing it. Mere factual errors need not harm our spiritual eyesight, even though they may cause us inconvenience. Why did Eve believe Satan? She believed him because *his lie was more appealing to her dawning lust and vanity than was God's truth.*

To cling feverishly to our innocence when we are really guilty or to feel perfectly safe when we are in danger is serious. We *feel better* when we deny something unpleasant, putting it out of our minds. But closing our eyes to reality does not make it go away. Believe a lie and our minds are darkened. We become fools. We walk, filled with false peace, towards a precipice.

We have the mind of Christ, but only as we walk in his light, as we face him who is the truth. Nothing could be more terrible than the blindness that falls as God's judgment on those to whom he once gave light.

A vision of darkness

I had a strange experience during an early-morning prayer meeting a few months ago. Call it a prophetic experience if you like. It was sudden and brief (no longer than ten seconds) but condensed and exceptionally powerful. We were praying together in our living room, and it was my turn to pray. I prayed, like the others, for an outpouring of God's Spirit over Canada and for revival. My prayer was earnest enough, for the theme was important to all of us.

As I prayed I was thinking about this blindness. Suddenly, and totally unexpectedly, I saw it. I mean, I saw the blindness, the judgment. It was as though a veil had been suddenly torn back to shock me with what it had hidden. I cannot describe what I saw, but it so appalled me that I struggled out of my soft armchair, crying , 'No, no! Don't do it! You mustn't. Stop! Stop!' I had raised my hand, like a police officer in traffic, as though I could stop the Almighty in his tracks.

Simultaneously – how could so much be registered in mere seconds? – I received the certain knowledge that some Christian leaders across the country (I have no idea who they might be) would not find repentance. They had hardened their hearts too much. They will remain blind to themselves and to what God is doing. But God will grant others, leaders and followers alike, profound repentance and contrition. And revival will follow. Time will reveal and others will judge the validity of my strange experience.

Jesus, quoting Isaiah on darkness of mind, affirms the phenomenon of 'judicial blindness':

'Though seeing, they do not see;
    though hearing, they do not hear or
        understand.

In them is fulfilled the prophecy of Isaiah:

'"You will be ever hearing but never
        understanding;
    you will be ever seeing but never
        perceiving.
For this people's heart has become calloused;
    they hardly hear with their ears,
    and they have closed their eyes.
Otherwise they might see with their eyes,
    hear with their ears,

195

understand with their hearts
and turn, and I would heal them."'
(Mt. 13:13–15)

Ezekiel also talks of this God-sent idiocy: 'But
they rebelled against me and would not listen to
me; they did not get rid of the vile images they had
set their eyes on, nor did they forsake the idols of
Egypt. So I said I would pour out my wrath on
them and spend my anger against them in Egypt.
... *I also gave them over to statutes that were not good
and laws they could not live by*' (Ezk. 20:8, 25).

What is Ezekiel saying? First, he affirms that God
eventually brings judgment to his rebellious
people. Ezekiel 20 is a moving testimony to God's
patience in the face of Israel's rebellious idolatry.
Again and again God restrains his anger. But when
he eventually acts, what form does his action take?

In effect he says, 'Very well, since you have
chosen to worship Baal and Moloch I will leave you
to discover the consequences for yourselves.' God
gave the Israelites over to the vile results of
worshipping foreign gods. They would be blind to
the stupidity of laws of their own making, '*statutes
that were not good and laws they could not live by*', in the
hope that they might discover by painful experience the folly of their choice.

We cannot think properly unless the one true
God is central to our thinking. We cannot think
straight unless he has mastered us. Like the
religious leaders of Christ's time, without God in
our midst our thinking becomes futile; we grow
stupid, obtuse. We may be brilliant in academic
performance, yet we are unable to see what is right
under our noses.

You remember Isaiah's awesome experience of seeing the Lord? He was commissioned to proclaim this sort of blindness, *which was to continue until the southern kingdom was taken captive*:

'[God] said, 'Go and tell this people:

"Be ever hearing, but never understanding;
    be ever seeing, but never perceiving."
Make the heart of this people calloused;
    make their ears dull
    and close their eyes.
Otherwise they might see with their eyes,
    hear with their ears,
    understand with their hearts,
and turn and be healed.'

Then I said, 'For how long, O Lord?'
And he answered:

'Until the cities lie ruined
    and without inhabitant,
until the houses are left deserted
    and the fields ruined and ravaged'

(Is. 6:9–11)

Lash 2: Idol worship is born

Once our minds have been darkened, God allows us to reap the harvest we have chosen. When we choose to ignore him, he gives us over to superstition. Idolatry represents the second phase of his judgment on human society. People become fools and exchange 'the glory of the immortal God for images made to look like mortal man and birds and animals and reptiles' (Rom. 1:23).

197

We Christians do not bow down to idols. It is not that we are godly, but that we are 'scientific'. We have been brainwashed to a much greater extent than we realize by the naturalism that pervades the twentieth century.[2] To science, idols reflect primitive superstition. Curiously, the prophets agree – that is, they depicted idols as carved pieces of wood and stone with no ability to perform magic, much less to answer prayer. However, behind the idol they saw the malign rule of ancient gods.

While they poured scorn on idols, the prophets were under no misapprehension about those 'other gods' and their worship. They never discussed the identity of the strange gods. Most of us assume they are fallen angels who still seek a claim on our loyalty, still lust for diabolical sovereignty over us. They are 'the powers of this dark world ... the spiritual forces of evil in the heavenly realms' (Eph. 6:12) to which I referred earlier. Either we wrestle against them or we bow unwittingly in worship to them, accepting their enslavement for the rewards they offer.

Now while we may not carve idols or bow down to them, we do in fact worship money, material things, sex and power. We refer to money as 'the bottom line' and try to find our level in society by the kind of houses, cars and furniture we possess. We also pander to our bodies. Yuppiness demands care with diet, exercise, hygiene and lotions – all very well in their place, but deadly when they crowd God out.

When we value money too highly, we begin to worship mammon, a spiritual power whose service is perilous. When we hanker after power itself, we begin to worship Satan. Who? Us? 'No way!' we say, which is precisely the response of every person whom God has given over to darkness. Darkness is that by which you cannot see yourself and the true nature of your actions.

To the degree that things like cash, sex and power govern our everyday behaviour, they interfere with true worship and bring us into bondage to dark powers. Secretly we begin to wonder why the gospel's power to deliver us from sinful habits no longer seems to work. Give Satan an inch and he claims his mile. The fact is, we have chosen values that lead us back into the very slavery Christ freed us from – the slavery of 'the dominion of darkness' (Col. 1:13). Like dogs, we return to our vomit, or like the Israelites, we lust helplessly for Egypt's garlic and onions.

Lash 3: Slaves to sexual perversion

Therefore we, like the pagans described in Romans 1 and ancient Israel, are 'given over' to sexual impurity, to shameful lusts and to a depraved mind (Rom. 1:24–28).

Notice that vulnerability to sexual sin is here *part of the judgment*. God gives us over to 'sexual impurity for the degrading of [our] bodies'! To put it another way, God, in an act of judgment, removes his divine protection against sexual sin and perversion. He removes it because we no longer know him as he wants to be known. So long as our behaviour has been governed by our pursuit of material well-being, or by the worship of our bodies and their sensations, he has allowed us to stumble proudly and blindly. We blunder along an idolatrous road of sin until we lose ourselves in a maze of sexual allurements.

I use the pronouns 'we' and 'us' advisedly. I insist – indeed, it has become utterly plain – that the church is in this case part of society. The judgment has also fallen upon us. One Christian leader after another falls into sexual sin, which also sweeps the rank and file of the church. As a former psychiatrist who sees many Christians, I know that the extent of sexual misbehaviour in the church now compares with what goes on in the world.

The research department of *Christianity Today* conducted two surveys among the magazine's readers. One concerned pastors' sexual habits and the other the sexual failures of lay people. The research department mailed out nearly two thousand questionnaires, divided equally between the two groups. Thirty per cent replied. The results confirm what some of us already knew.

Question 2 of the questionnaire to pastors read, 'Have you ever had sexual intercourse with someone other than your spouse since you've been in local church ministry?' Twelve per cent answered yes, and eighty-eight per cent no. Of the latter, many indicated that their purity had not come easily.

Eighteen per cent of the pastors admitted to passionate kissing, fondling, mutual masturbation, and the like. Such pastors are troubled to make their admissions, but many have no-one to turn to for help and counsel.

The report continues, 'Incidences of immorality [among the laity] were nearly double: 45% indicated having done something sexually inappropriate, 23% said they had had extramarital intercourse, and 28% said they had engaged in other forms of extramarital sexual conduct.[3]

I must not give the impression that we are supposed to be immune to temptation. Yet the picture the statistics show is not intended to be the norm in the church. Holiness should be the norm. It is part of the judgment that has fallen on us. Francis Frangipane, a US charismatic leader, comments, 'There are respectable men who love God and seek to serve Him, yet secretly in their hearts they are prisoners of Jezebel. Even now they are deeply ashamed of their bondage to pornography; and they can barely control their desires for women. Ask them to pray and their spirits are awash with guilt and shame. Their prayers are but the whimpers of Jezebel's eunuchs.'[4]

It now grows clearer that hard-core porn is the major factor in recent increases in rape, sexual cruelty and murder. Unhappily, we begin to see the terrible end-products of depravity, as Paul lists them in Romans 1, both in contemporary society and in church members.

Sadly, Christian sexual failures do not confine themselves to heterosexual activity. Homosexual practices (overt and in secret, to say nothing of the struggle against homosexual impulses) are widespread.

Statistics in countries other than the United States may differ, but I question whether they differ much. Pastors all over the world report grave concern about the extent of esoteric forms of promiscuity among Christians. But please note: the current weakness of Christians in the face of the world's impurity *is itself an expression of God's*

201

judgment. God has 'given us over' to sexual vulner-ability. Far from excusing our sexual lapses, this should only draw our attention to our deeper sin, the sin of not honouring him as God in the way we conduct our lives.

Lash 4: Disease

Christians all over the world are falling into every form of sexual perversion and immorality. Ever stronger, antibiotic-resistant strains of herpes, gonorrhoea and syphilis appear and spread yearly. Aids is the latest in a series of sexually transmitted diseases. We have 'received ... the due penalty' for tolerating sexual perversion in our midst. For Aids is not primarily a judgment of God against homosexuals. After all, it has now many other victims, including wives who had no idea what was happening and children too young to know, some still in the womb. It is a judgment of God against a society he has allowed to reap a whirlwind.

The result is the sexual insanity into which our pride has led us. And it is the sexual insanity that is the real judgment. Aids is merely the result, the final working out of the judgment.

Lash 5: The approach to catastrophe

The last five verses of Romans 1 describe the fifth lash of earthly judgment. They present an appal-ling picture. Yet it is a picture of human behaviour that we see all around us.

Furthermore, *since they did not think it worth while to retain the knowledge of God*, he gave them over to a depraved mind, to do what ought not to be done. They have become filled with every kind of wickedness, evil, greed and depravity. They are full of envy, murder, strife, deceit and malice. They are gossips, slanderers, God-haters, insolent, arrogant and boastful; they invent ways of doing evil; they disobey their parents; they are senseless, faithless, heartless, ruthless. *Although they know God's righteous decree that those who do such things deserve death*, they not only continue to do these very things but also approve of those who practise them (Rom. 1:28–32).

I have underlined two phrases in the passage above. Both emphasize the point Paul insists on. Blindness to the things of God is deliberate blindness, for which all human beings in every part of the globe, saved or unsaved, evangelized or unevangelized, educated or not, are responsible. We *chose* blindness when we turned from God.

The picture Paul paints is of a society in the throes of sinful disintegration. It is also a picture of infantile defiance towards God. We are children who foolishly defy the heavenly Father. Our defiance is exemplified in William Henley's famous poem, 'Invictus':

> Out of the night that covers me,
> Black as the Pit from pole to pole,
> I thank whatever gods may be
> For my unconquerable soul . . .

It matters not how strait the gate,
How charged with punishments the scroll,
I am the master of my fate:
I am the captain of my soul.

The behaviour Paul describes and the attitude
Henley exults in are not only Satanic but also
infinitely childish. No laughter echoes from
heaven. God weeps, weeps in longing and love at
the tragedy of fools who proudly ape gods. This is
the society we live in. These are the influences
invading the church and even our own hearts.

In past ages the initial lashes of the whip of
judgment were not enough to turn people from
their stubborn course, so that worse judgments
followed – the kind conjured up in our minds by
John's vision of the four horses of the Apocalypse.
Nonetheless, God calls upon us to change our
ways and seek his mercy. That is the topic of the
next two chapters.

Chapter Fourteen

God's plea for his people

'Plead with your mother, plead' (Ho. 2:2, RSV).

More than once I have walked with a forsaken husband round his deserted house. Each time, by coincidence, night has made darkness darker and emptiness more hollow. Each time the man's voice was flat, incredulous, bewildered. 'It's funny. You know, I can't believe it's happened.' Then, pensively, 'The children's beds are all gone. She must have had it organized somehow.' Or, 'She's left my books and records and taken her own.' Or, 'She's taken all the kids' pictures.' Some litter usually lay around. A forgotten toy would be in a corner. We would mechanically empty the rubbish and check on the contents of the refrigerator. I remember sitting down on an old settee with one man. 'What shall I do, John? What shall I do?'

Perhaps from the bitterness of her heart a wife

could have given a fitting reply. I am not trying to take up cudgels on behalf of deserted husbands. Wives, too, are deserted every day to experience similar shock and pain. It is to pain I point. 'Plead with your mother, *plead*. . . .' As numbness wears off, an agony of longing makes itself felt. 'I would do anything, *anything*. . . . I can see I've been at fault, made many mistakes. But this seems so final.'

Hosea may or may not have made mistakes. We are not told. But God, whose voice we are now listening to, made none. 'Plead, *plead*.' God pleading? God feeling pain?

Whenever I have been involved with a deserted husband or wife, I have noticed something else. Once the decision is made, the deserter (man or woman) finds ways to avoid being exposed to the pain of the person deserted. Distance. No address. A sudden, well-planned departure with a curt, cold note about communication via a lawyer. An unlisted phone number. At all costs and by all means, the deserter must be shielded from the sights and sounds of wounds he or she has inflicted.

In fact, the preparation to ward off pain has sometimes been taking place for months. Psychological as well as physical barriers have been constructed. 'I don't feel anything for him now.' 'I just don't love her any more.' 'There's nothing there. It's all over between us.'

So the deserted party is doubly cut off, logistically and psychologically. Into a blank wall a heart cries with inarticulate pleading, echoed but unheard.

Two things puzzle us about God's grief over his

206

people. In the first place we find it hard to believe that God should be upset about our materialism. We are also puzzled that God should feel the pain of desertion. He is self-sufficient, infinite. He has no needs. He pours out riches without lessening anything of what he has or is. We can contribute nothing which will add a jot to him.

Yet he pleads, feels pain, cries out with longing. Cries to a church that has shielded herself from his pain, a church that refuses to look into his weeping eyes or that feels a strange emptiness where love once burned. If there is a wonder greater than God reduced to a helpless infant in a barn, it is the wonder of an infinite God torn with an agony of longing for a people that has forsaken him and that has no awareness of his pain.

Of course these wonders are one. The cry, 'Plead, plead'; the kicking, swaddled infant; the tortured form, racked in darkness on a gibbet: all three are one. In all three we see the marvel of God's pain because of a harlot.

It is pain for the harlot's fate, not pain for himself. Pain lest he do what he must do, 'strip her naked . . . and slay her with thirst' (Ho. 2:3).

'Therefore I will take away my grain when it
    ripens,
   and my new wine when it is ready.
I will take back my wool and my linen,
   intended to cover her nakedness.
So now I will expose her lewdness
   before the eyes of her lovers;
   no-one will take her out of my hands.'
                                    (Hos. 2:9–10)

Our problem with a punitive God is that we are ourselves bitter and vindictive. 'It hurts me more than it hurts you' has a hollow ring from human lips. God's agony, on the other hand, is free of venom. It is agony beyond anything we can understand, but agony he feels on our behalf. He knows, because he is holy, what he must do. Holiness and love clash fiercely so that fires rage in his bosom, selfless fires in a God of holiness and love. He takes no pleasure in stripping, in starving, in exposing. He has no joy in the death of the wicked, only an infinite pain.

Yet he will do what he must. His attitude to sin is inflexible. He will not stay his hand, however long he may delay it. He will warn, threaten, plead. But finally he will act, and when he does his judgments will be as thorough as they are unswerving. It has been so throughout the Scripture and throughout church history, and it will remain so till the end of time.

So when he pleads with the western church, he does so because of what he can see lying ahead of us, not only for those of us who are leaders and therefore more responsible, but for those who are our children and have followed us. 'Upon her children also I will have no pity' (Ho. 2:4).

Children don't always realize what is happening to start with. Even when they do and cry, 'Where is Mummy? I want Mummy!' they soon learn to suppress the longings of their little hearts. They learn that in some obscure sense the missing parent is now the enemy. If you want to keep the affection of the parent you still have, you learn (even if you are only four or five years old) to be relatively discreet about your feelings towards the enemy.

So it is the children (as we are reminded time without number) who suffer. And historically it has always seemed that the judgments of God appear to fall indiscriminately upon villains and their offspring. When foreign armies overran Israel or Judah, the heads of little ones would be dashed against the rocks, the women raped, the aged tossed over a precipice.

We are sickened by the horror of it all and avoid those pages of Scripture which implicate God's judgments in such atrocities. We prefer to worship a different god, made up of our favourite selections from Scripture. Many Bible scholars have grappled with moral problems of God's divine judgment through the historical process, and I will not add here to what they have said except to say that there are things more important than physical survival.

Hosea's only comment concerns *why* God's judgment falls on children of harlotry. It is because they are just that, children of harlotry. Just as David's first child with Bathsheba died, so will many of our own. And if we pause to think for a moment, we may see that should God's judgment fall upon the twentieth-century church, it must inevitably fall on many who have been conceived in idolatry and fed on the milk of materialistic unbelief. Like mother, like daughter; like father, like son. We have reared a brood of children who are ours but who may not, whatever they profess with their lips, be children of God at all. Evangelical churches, fundamentalist churches, liberal Protestant and Catholic churches are full of people who have gone through some form of Christianization (be it

209

baptism or going forward) but whom we have taught to trust in money and in technology more than in the ascended Christ.

Values changed by adversity

But our God is a God of mercy. Even his punishments have restoration in mind.

> 'Therefore I will block her path with
> thornbushes;
> I will wall her in so that she cannot find
> her way.
> She will chase after her lovers but not catch
> them. . . .
> Then she will say,
> "I will go back to my husband as at first,
> for then I was better off than now."'
>
> (Ho. 2:6–7)

It is curious how pain, adversity and danger can change our values. I met a man who was trapped for hours in the cabin of an overturned eighteen-wheel truck. Fuel had dripped over him as he lay there helplessly. Cold and snow reduced his chances of rescue. And even when he was found, there was the drawn-out problem of getting him free.

How many thoughts raced through his mind! Things that had seemed of paramount importance hours before suddenly became of no account. The foolish urge to deliver his goods on time. Personal relationships. Time itself and how to use it. What life was for. What he would do with twenty-four hours of freedom if he could have them.

When eventually he stood on his feet, free, uninjured, staring at the half-buried wreckage, he was staring at a life that no longer existed. It lay with the ruins of the truck. He was a changed man, seeing things as he had never seen them before. And his new vision corresponded with truer values than his old one. Pain and danger had led him to truth.

Chuck Colson tells in his book *Born Again* how the pressures of Watergate and even the dehumanization of prison totally changed his perspective on life and were used by God to draw him into a tender love relationship with him. The same story could be repeated with a thousand variations. It is not that adversity merely changes our behaviour. It changes the way we see things. And our new vision can be a doorway to joy, to peace, to unimaginable liberty. There are signs of repentance and longing in some compromising churches under oppressive governments.

The devil, of course, has his deadly counterfeit of the same process by which pain changes our view of life. A political prisoner is thrown in jail. She cannot sleep in her cell, for the lights glare, and she is awakened at irregular intervals. At times she is dragged and roughly thrust into the presence of accusing officials, who bully her with threats, frighten her with a surprising knowledge of her past life, dismay her by showing her a letter from her husband (perhaps a forged one) telling her he has left her for someone else. She may be subject to torture or beatings and be left half-starved with no medical attention.

But then, unexpectedly comes kindness – the mild, understanding official, offering a cigarette, solicitous about all the prisoner has been through, showing her that she is a tragic victim of heartless capitalistic imperialism. The prisoner, too, begins to see things differently. The world she once believed in grows strangely unreal, distorted. A new set of ideas suddenly seems obvious, real. Why had she never understood before? It all seems so clear, now.

Is God a washer of brains?

There are profound differences between the God of the prophets and political brainwashers. God has no interest in manipulating results. He could, if he so desired, change our life-view by a snap of his fingers. He would have no need to resort to a play on our feelings. By a simple word he could make us insane so that we would say black was white and red was green.

But he does not need techniques and equipment. He is not a manipulator. He proved that when he gave us the power to choose.

Moreover, his tenderness is not fake. It is not an act designed to play on our weakness but the revelation of his very heart. And when we will let him, he does not turn us over to an underling but condescends to draw near himself. Finally he is interested in truth. He is truth. His only object is to help us see the truth. Seeing the truth, we can make a meaningful choice. Acting on truth will make us free.

'Therefore, I am now going to allure her ... and speak tenderly to her' (Ho. 2:14). The picture is a beautiful one. To woo is not to seduce. The seducer plays on feelings to gain a selfish end; the lover woos to overcome those fears that prevent a lost woman from becoming a princess. The seducer manipulates; the wooer shows genuine kindness and understanding. The seducer yearns to get; the wooer, to give.

Yet in each case the process is a delicate one. It must be gentle, for it is resisted by fear and mistrust. And the fear is understandable. God is a God of fiery rage. What we do not see is that this rage concerns our sin. His tenderness concerns ourselves. Because we are human, we are nervous about this untamed God of fire. We are wild birds needing to learn trust. We neither see what is there nor hear what is said. If we are Beauty, we can see only the Beast. We may have heard his stern denunciations, but we have never learned to hear the music of a love that passes knowledge.

Is it not a marvel that God should take time to woo? 'Take it or leave it,' says the rich film star who offers a wedding ring to a starlet. And if she takes the ring, she finds she has to take it off a year later. Yet here comes one who loves us with an everlasting love and who is in no hurry. He takes time. He speaks gently. If his wooing becomes urgent, it never ceases to be tender. But it may not be until we have suffered that our eyes are open to see, our ears to hear, our hearts to feel.

The door of restoration

'I will ... make the Valley of Achor a door of hope' (Ho. 2:15). I cannot, I suppose, address the church as a whole, but only you who read. The Valley of Achor was a valley where terrible judgment fell on Achan and his family (Jos. 7:20–26). We shudder to read of wholesale burning and stoning, and the pile of rocks heaped over the charred bones of those on whom God's judgment fell. We wonder how fair it was that Achan's family should have suffered as well. But we must be realists rather than moralists. Our actions do affect others. A father's unwise speculations reduce his family to poverty, or his alcoholism may subject them to violence, hunger and fear. Not that God would have it so. He deplores the fact that children suffer for their parents' sins (Ezk. 18). However, you yourself may be facing, even now, not only the personal pain of the Lord's discipline but also the unspoken agony of being responsible for the fact that his judgments affect those most dear to you.

The Valley of Achor is intended to be a door of hope. God's object is to restore his relationship with you. Until that relationship is restored, you cannot heal the pain of others. Only one who is healed can heal. And God waits to draw near to you. He waits to turn dryness into streams of water and flower-filled meadows, to turn loneliness into fellowship, purposelessness into purpose, emptiness into fullness of joy. The very catastrophe that may have fallen on you is itself your greatest opportunity if only you will see it.

Review your position. Review your priorities. What have you been insisting on so fiercely? What is the something you have vowed never to give way on? Are you so sure you are right in the stand you have taken? You *may* be, but is God trying to shed new light on your circumstances? Take time to weigh matters again. Do not be afraid of what you may have to let go. Expose yourself, if you have to, to the humiliation of being in the wrong. So you have been a fool or worse. So people will smile and say, 'I always said he was wrong!' You are not the first.

The door of hope in the Valley of Achor may have a low lintel. Bow your head a little as you step through. The new world into which you will pass will soon dissolve your humiliations in a deeper joy than you have yet known. A. W. Tozer wrote in his book *The Pursuit of God*,

Before the Lord God made man upon the earth He first prepared for him by creating a world of useful and pleasant things for his sustenance and delight. In the Genesis account of the creation these are called simply 'things'. They were made for man's uses, but they were meant always to be external to the man and subservient to him. In the deep heart of the man was a shrine where none but God was worthy to come. Within him was God; without, a thousand gifts which God had showered upon him.

But sin has introduced complications and has made those very gifts of God a potential source of ruin to the soul.

Our woes began when God was forced out of His central shrine and 'things' were allowed to enter. Within the human heart 'things' have taken over. Men have now by nature no peace within their hearts, for God is crowned there no longer, but there in the moral dusk stubborn and aggressive usurpers fight among themselves for first place on the throne.

How do we rid ourselves of those 'stubborn and aggressive usurpers' that fight in the moral dusk 'among themselves for first place on the throne'?

I remember, on a night some years ago, pacing the length of a beautiful tropical beach and crying out to God to be delivered from the power of mammon for ever. God has answered and is still answering my prayer. Things still attract me, but I now know what I really want. Tozer also wrote,

> The man who has God for his treasure has all things in One. Many ordinary treasures may be denied him, or if he is allowed to have them, the enjoyment of them will be so tempered that they will never be necessary to his happiness. Or if he must see them go, one after one, he will scarcely feel a sense of loss, for having the Source of all things he has in One all satisfaction, all pleasure, all delight. Whatever he may lose he has actually lost nothing, for he now has it all in One, and he has it purely, legitimately and forever.[1]

A choice faces you. There is not room for two treasures in your heart. Which will you choose?

Chapter Fifteen

The glory of repentance

I have always struggled against personal pride. That is understandable, since on both my parents' sides I am descended from well-known people. I get the tendency to pride from one of these – a female ancestor, way back in our family tree. One day she had an occult encounter. In fact, she encountered Satan himself, who gave her some interesting food, saying it would make her as knowledgeable as God himself (Gn. 3:5). The moment she ate it, Satan successfully infected her with the virus that had led to his downfall, and pride was born in her. It has troubled every member of our family since. It is the deepest root of sin in me.

Pride: the prime and primal sin

Pride is, of course, the starting point of every kind of evil, the sin from which all ugliness spreads. It began with Satan, who then seduced Eve by telling her she would be 'like God'. C. S. Lewis puts the matter interestingly: 'Unchastity, anger, greed, drunkenness and all that, are mere fleabites in comparison: it was through Pride that the devil became the devil: Pride leads to every other vice: it is the complete anti-God state of mind.'[1]

Pride is the primary problem of the Christian church. If, as I believe, materialism is the key sin in the West, then pride is its antecedent. We need to repent of our pride even more than of our materialism, since the one parents the other. Pride arouses God's wrath and hatred more than any other sin – wrath against the proud, hatred against the sin. 'To fear the LORD is to hate evil; I [wisdom] hate pride and arrogance, evil behaviour and perverse speech' (Pr. 8:13).

Pride is the first item of a list of items that God finds detestable: 'There are six things the LORD hates, seven that are detestable to him: haughty eyes, a lying tongue, hands that shed innocent blood . . .' (Pr. 6:16–17).

Yet denominational pride was the first thing my young heart picked up in church. It thrives in churches, hideously blooming in quarrels, arrogantly asserting itself in material display. My earliest experiences were in a small Plymouth Brethren assembly, and one that was not necessarily typical of all Brethren assembles. I appreciate to this day the godliness, the adherence to Scripture, the true sense of worship that I learned even as a child.

As a child too, however, I picked up the proud notion that while there certainly might be other

Christians apart from us, they unfortunately belonged to things called 'sects and schisms and denominations.' We were neither a sect nor a schism, nor yet a denomination. We had separated ourselves *from* all sects, schisms and denominations. We were just Christians. We had nothing to learn from the rest. In fact, their doctrines were dangerous. So we praised God that we had been gathered together in the name of the Lord, and that we had 'come out from among them' and were separate. We would not 'touch ... the unclean thing'.

Do I sound cynical? To be quite frank, it is easier for me to strike a cynical pose than to let myself feel. I begin at times to catch a glimpse of the real nature of what we have let Satan do to churches, as well as of the judgment that is coming. I am frightened, not so much of God (though of him too) as of looking at what has happened and allowing myself to see its horror. We have grown so accustomed to pride that we no longer feel it, much less perceive its evil.

Since my childhood I have had a lifetime of experience in interdenominational organizations. This has brought me experience of a wide variety of denominational churches. Not all of the groups use such uncompromising terms to express their unique and blessed call as the small Brethren assembly of my boyhood, but all have subtle variants of the same notion. Rare is the Christian group not guilty of the sin which Lewis calls 'the complete anti-God state of mind' and the sin by which the devil became the devil.

Pride among evangelicals

Ironically, church pride always seems to succeed a period of heroic church faithfulness, of meriting God's 'Well done!' in an exceptional way. I think of myself as a conservative evangelical. I don't know that the adjective 'conservative' was applied to evangelicalism before the advent of German liberal scholarship, a scholarship undermining Scripture's authority. My spiritual forebears pleased God. They determined to honour God's Word, believing it to be just that. Scripture's authority and inspiration were critical then, and remain so today.

They did not fight because they were proud, and certainly not because they were materialists. The 'new' theology quickly became more fashionable than the old, for that is the way fashions work. In resisting fashion, my forebears faced the humiliation of having poorer appointments in the universities and theological colleges. Often they settled for smaller churches and meagre salaries. Their colleagues despised them for their convictions. They paid a heavy price, losing status and income. Faithfulness costs.

From the outset the conservatives, knowing they had nothing to fear by doing so, gave themselves increasingly to documentary and linguistic research. They produced papers, wrote biblical and theological works and established presses, as well as their own theological and Bible colleges. Eventually they were accepted on the basis of their scholastic competence and were able to compete for higher academic posts in top teaching centres *while still proving faithful to Scripture.*

Somewhere along the road, weeds of pride began to grow – pride in our heritage, pride in our scholarship, publishing enterprises and prosperous institutions, pride in being conservative evangelicals. Pride began to undermine a simple confidence in God. Our scholarship impressed some of us so much that we began to trust scholarship itself, to trust exegetical skill and hermeneutical sophistication more than God's Spirit to reveal the will of God in Scripture. And along with the pride came a half-conscious awareness of the importance of money and property. Once willing to sacrifice financial security and status, we never detected the moment when tiny shoots of greed and acquisitiveness began to appear among the blossoms of our gratitude. We took pride in having achieved both intellectual respectability and solid, wealthy institutions.

Then in 1904 in Wales, and in 1906 in the States, the Holy Spirit birthed another evangelical movement which could hardly be labelled conservative or scholastically sophisticated – at least in its first years. Early *Los Angeles Times* reports of the movement's beginnings are astonishing, if derisory. Yet since God for a special reason chooses the foolish, the movement spread rapidly.

At that point we conservatives, alarmed by the vigour and claims of the new movement, denied our own relative powerlessness and began to fight on two fronts, against liberalism and against Pentecostalism. We may even have been in peril of that sin that cannot be forgiven. We belittled the very real power for which the movement became a channel, power to win souls, power to heal the sick. We denied that it was the Holy Spirit's power. Was not Pentecostal doctrine in error? I believe that in some points it was. But God gives power in response to obedience rather than in response to doctrinal purity, important as the latter may be.

From the outset the Pentecostals were fervently evangelistic. Consisting largely of those looked down upon both by well-educated people and by established churches, the Pentecostal movement spread among the poor and working classes. The gospel, increasingly the prerogative of the middle classes and the more educated, was again being preached to the poor. The astonishing growth of churches and of truly repentant and converted people testified that the Holy Spirit's power accounted for the movement's success. Like members of many movements before, they faced derision and even persecution, the latter not official, but by critics and jeerers. Pentecostals seemed to thrive on it.

Inevitable signs of upward mobility appeared. Respectability became important. Since membership was warm and generous, money began to flow. Not only did it flow into missions, but into Bible colleges and, in North America, denominational schools and seminaries. And there was nothing wrong with that. Publications grew in volume, variety and sophistication. Wealth appeared and flourished. Worship showed distinct tendencies towards professionalism. Did not all this prosperity indicate that God was showing which groups had spiritual power? Perhaps. But have Pentecostals forgotten the lessons of their earliest years – the years when they spread even more rapidly in North America than they do now? Where was the movement's deepest confidence in those days? In institutions? In property? In schools? The trouble about God's gifts to us is that we so quickly trust them, rather than him.

Pride, pride that grieves God, had infected that branch too, just as it had infected every other branch of the evangelical community, conservative, charismatic or whatever. We all forget our beginnings. We all accept the costly heritage that has come down to us, forgetting that we never paid the price for it. *We* are better off financially because *they* accepted low pay. *We* enjoy the respect of our neighbours while *they* endured scorn. Yet the price we have paid for our respectability is a far bigger one than they paid for their faithfulness. We have lost God's smile and are too blind to recognize the fact.

What begins in a movement as courageous willingness to suffer any loss, any derision, for Christ, becomes something more acceptable both to society in general and to the religious community in particular. Respectability is measured by time (the length of your history), by learning and, to a lesser degree, by property. We settle down slowly, accepting our place in society and in the denominational pecking order, each making sure everyone knows that we are not without our reasons to take pride in our particular heritage.

Learning from the Pharisees

There are lessons from history that we never learn. Two centuries before Christ the Jews were ruled by Antiochus IV, the so-called Antiochus Epiphanes. An insane tyrant, Antiochus did all he could to stamp out their faith. He reputedly

223

amputated the breasts of Jewish mothers who had their sons circumcised. As is commonly the case, there were two reactions to his tyranny – resistance and collaboration.

Many scholars believe that pharisaism had its roots at this time. The forerunners of the Pharisees determined to adhere to the law and the prophets, and to be faithful in all things to their God – a very dangerous and courageous stance to take. They were doing in perilous times what conservative evangelicals and Pentecostals alike did during the less perilous times of the last two centuries. We did not face imprisonment and death, but we did face ridicule, and in some cases, academic and denominational obscurity.

Courage in time of adversity often becomes self-congratulation and self-righteous pride in less troubled times. This proved to be so in the case of the Pharisees. It is understandable that two hundred years later the attitude of the Pharisees should have changed. In New Testament times they earned Christ's repeated condemnation. His denunciation of the Pharisees in Matthews 23 appalls us by its ferocity; his interchanges with them in John 5, 7 and 8 shock us by their harsh dealings. Jesus condemned the Pharisees not for their knowledge of the Bible, but for their blind unwillingness to see what they had done with the knowledge their forebears had died to preserve. Equally understandably, our history has taken the same turn as that of the Pharisees. We need to repent, and to repent soon.

Repentance: a neglected doctrine

Two weeks ago I found myself in the Canadian

224

Maritimes. I had seen true repentance break out more than once in a public meeting, but had never observed the phenomenon when I preached. It had occurred to people in the hours and days following my having preached about repentance (for God is bringing repentance with increasing frequency these days) on several occasions, but never during the meeting.

Curiously, I had been asked to speak about repentance on this occasion, but chose not to. The Holy Spirit had impressed me with the knowledge that people in the area were more than usually gripped with sexual sin, some as aggressors, others as victims. So instead, I took sexual sin as my theme. From the moment I began I sensed an unusual power, a power which had nothing to do with me or the way I preached. God was doing something. Yet I would not say that I exerted any emotional pressure. I would describe the atmosphere in the meeting as one of alertness, yet calm. Soon a woman on the front row began to sob and continued to do so intermittently for the whole address, comforted by the woman beside her.

As I concluded I asked those who were in the grip of sexual sins to come to the front of the auditorium for counselling and prayer. A very large number came, crowding the area around the platform. After asking counsellors to come forward too, I prayed aloud that God would minister by his Holy Spirit to each one as they needed it. Then we stood together quietly in God's presence.

Several people began to weep. Soon the sound of sobbing, wailing and bitter cries filled the auditorium. Many of those who had come forward were trembling violently. I was filled with a sense of awe, recognizing with absolute clarity that a work of God was in progress that owed nothing to my influence in the meeting. In many people profound repentance was taking place. The tender love of God was being manifested to sinners.

God is certainly a God of justice and of judgment. He is, after all, a holy God. But of greater importance still, his nature is one of love. He *is* love. That is, the most basic component in his holiness is that of love. We can perceive (and even then only dimly) each attribute – of holiness and of love – only in the light of the other. The more we grasp his holy abhorrence and detestation of sin, the greater we will wonder at his love. Several times in recent months I have cried aloud in profound perplexity and wonder, 'How can you *possibly* love me?' It is at this point that worship arises, repentance begins and the deepest kind of church renewal starts.

What can one person do about the church's need for repentance? No-one has the power to make it happen, either to themselves or to anyone else. Isn't this a matter for leaders to look at? I'm sure it is. Christian leaders should take a lead. They should be calling on the rest of us to humble ourselves before God, to acknowledge our blindness and our spiritual poverty. But this in itself will not bring repentance, only an acknowledgment that we need it. And we who are not leaders need not wait till leaders do this. So what can we do?

We must do two things. One is to ask God to search our hearts by his Spirit, acknowledging our sin as he does so. To indulge in self-righteous criticism and judgment of the church is wrong. What if the church, our mother, turns out to be a whore? The fact is painful, and the pain great, but we are not called on to spurn or to abandon her, to add division to division, quarrel to quarrel. We are called to pray both for her and for ourselves.

We are to pray for her with pure hearts and much faith. To do that we need God to sort out our lives. We, too, need repentance. Therefore, having acknowledged our sin and need, we must ask God to *give* us repentance in his own time and way. Heart-searching and confession are a start.

As we pray also for the church around us, we must pray *as a part of her*. We assume the burden of her sins on our shoulders, confessing them as our own. We *identify with* the church, for we are part of her. Her sins are our own. Is that biblical? You bet it is! Read Nehemiah 1 and Daniel 9. Daniel and Nehemiah were righteous men. Their righteousness stands out against the backdrop of the infidelity of the southern kingdom. Yet notice how they prayed for their nation. It was not *I and they*, but *I*, *myself and we*.

We have sinned and done wrong. We have been wicked and have rebelled; we have turned away from your commands and laws. We have not listened to your servants the prophets, who spoke in your name to our kings, our princes and our fathers, and to all the people of the land (Dn. 9:5–6).

I confess the sins we Israelites, including myself and my father's house, have committed against you. We have acted very

wickedly toward you. We have not obeyed
the commands, decrees and laws you gave
your servant Moses (Ne. 1:6–7).

If we want a spirit of repentance to be poured
out on the church we must plead from within her,
not from afar.

The nature of repentance

I have never, to my knowledge, heard a sermon on
repentance. What I have read on the subject has
nearly all been in books of more than a hundred
years old. We have references to repentance in
books and sermons, but we lack a precise knowledge of what it is. Theologians and Bible scholars
define it as a turning – a turning *to* God *from* sin. (It
seems that in the Bible the two concepts, of conversion and repentance, overlap somewhat.)

Problems remain, however. The repentance
people described in older books seems to involve
weeping, or at least a surprising degree of
emotion, just as in the meeting I described. Were
people then different from us? The Bible does talk
about *contrition*, sorrow for sin. What role (if any)
should emotion play in repentance? Is the definition I just quoted inadequate in some way?

Well, yes and no. It adequately describes the end
result of repentance, but it hardly reflects its profound nature. The Scriptures talk about weeping.
The Jews wept as they listened to Ezra and others
reading the Bible. They wept in repentance as they
saw how far they had departed from God's law:

Then Nehemiah the governor, Ezra the
priest and scribe, and the Levites who were

228

instructing the people said to them all, 'This day is sacred to the LORD your God. Do not mourn or weep.' For all the people had been weeping as they listened to the words of the Law' (Ne. 8:9).

Paul discusses the relationship between sorrow and repentance:

> Yet now I am happy, not because you were made sorry, but because your sorrow led you to repentance. For you became sorrowful as God intended and so were not harmed in any way by us. Godly sorrow brings repentance that leads to salvation and leaves no regret, but worldly sorrow brings death. See what this godly sorrow has produced in you: what earnestness, what eagerness to clear yourselves, what indignation, what alarm, what longing, what concern, what readiness to see justice done. At every point you have proved yourselves to be innocent in this matter (2 Cor. 7:9–11).

Note three significant principles in the passage. First, sorrow leads to repentance (v. 9). It is a sorrow that God intends we should experience. Second, sorrow can either be worldly sorrow or godly sorrow, the worldly kind being associated with death (v. 10), the godly kind with changed behaviour. Third, sorrow associated with repentance is accompanied by fruits – earnestness, indignation (at oneself, and over wrongs done to others) and alarm (presumably over what one has

229

done). In other words, repentance is something more than acknowledging my fault, more even than turning from it. *It is that which initiates the turning*.

There is something called godly sorrow then. If it happened to the Corinthians because of their sin, it should happen to us over our sins. If it should not happen to us when we sin, then what we have labelled repentance may not be what the Bible calls repentance. Indeed there are profound reasons why godly sorrow is essential to normal Christian living.

It is obvious to me as a psychiatrist that the most profound behavioural changes – and the most enduring – are those associated with deep emotion. We cannot, however, manipulate or produce emotions. Good actors can weep as in playing a role, but that sort of weeping is not godly sorrow. Nor is weeping because we see what a mess our actions have got us into. That is what Paul called worldly sorrow.

So what *is* godly sorrow? It is neither superficial, sentimental nor selfish. Godly sorrow is a product of illumination by the Holy Spirit.[2] It is a 'seeing' that only the Holy Spirit can give, a new view of our sin and our Saviour. It represents true knowing. It is possible to know facts in our heads that never grip us as people. In chapter six I discussed desensitization. We have been desensitized to sin, to God's wrath, to God's love.

In the same way we may 'know' that to be involved in a serious car accident can be an emotionally devastating event, yet be unmoved by the 'knowledge'. But to hit a car head on and survive with serious injuries gives us a different kind of knowledge. Even to watch an accident close up, or to have a near miss ourselves, shakes most of us profoundly.

We talk about knowing something 'in our hearts' when we experience its full impact. For most of us words like *sin*, *hell* and *lost* are words we can define, but that make little or no impact on our emotions. Again, we are desensitized to them. It is heart knowledge rather than head knowledge that leads to repentance. Only thus can profound and permanent behavioural changes take place, changes that do not reflect surface reformation, but that spring from a changed and healed spirit.

Jean LaFrance tells us, 'You may know the sins you have committed – failings in observing a rule or an established order, but that does not mean you have a sense of sin. The recognition of your sins stirs up in you a remorseful conscience and a guilty feeling, but not true repentance.'[3] If remorseful feelings alone change our behaviour God has not yet done the deep work he longs to do.

Only the Holy Spirit can show us the kind of video of our sin that has us crying out loud for mercy. Light of that sort shatters our calm. As God imparts a devastating interior illumination, we see our sins with appalling clarity, and as we never before have seen them. Weeping at the sight of them is not produced by skill in preaching, but by the illumination of the Holy Spirit who imparts a 'seeing' – a vision which shakes men and women to the depths of their being, and which *alone* can produce saving faith.

More important, he gives a revelation of the love of God in Christ. In fact it is the revelation of his love that is more likely to make us weep. When God himself shows us our sin we may find our mouths dry, our hearts pounding. We may be afraid, sleepless. Some people groan. But when in addition he reveals his love, then we weep with relief, with wonder, with adoration. Suddenly we know deep within us that this is the love we have hungered for all our lives, and now it is here.

A deep heart-knowledge of the love and the kindness of God awakens the emotions of repentance. Paul writes: 'Or do you show contempt for the riches of his kindness, tolerance and patience, not realising that God's kindness leads you towards repentance?' (Rom. 2:4).

Jean LaFrance, writing about repentance, declares: 'The discovery of your sin does not come from introspection, but from the contemplation of Christ on the cross.'[4] And Rees Howells, in describing the repentance he experienced on hearing a Jewish preacher talk about the cross, agrees: 'As Maurice Reuben brought those sacred scenes before us, I too saw the Cross. It seemed I spent ages at the Saviour's feet, and I wept and wept. I felt as if he had died just for me. I lost myself. . . . He broke me, and everything in me went right out to him.[5]

Some people weep too much, 'turning the tap on' at the drop of a hat. Others of us take pride in the fact that we do not weep. Yet others lament their inability to weep. Let us be sure of two things. First, our tear ducts would atrophy if we were not meant to use them. God gave them to us, crafting them himself with a purpose in mind. Second, we should weep in response to the importance of what we weep about. If we do not weep over our sin and Christ's love there is something profoundly wrong with us.

God and repentance

You may say: Wait a minute, doesn't the Bible *tell* us to repent? If so, doesn't that also imply that repenting is something we can do ourselves? In that case no special work of the Holy Spirit is called for. All we need is a will devoted to doing God's will.

This is true; however, true repentance – the kind initiated by the Holy Spirit – produces permanent behavioural changes. In the past I have found myself repenting of the same sin over and over again. Sometimes when I was tempted unbearably, I would sigh and give way to its delights, knowing that 'I can always repent and ask forgiveness anyway.' Such repentance is not repentance. With true repentance comes true faith, the kind of faith that brings both a deep heart-awareness of being forgiven, and the power to change.

Somehow our suspicions arise at this point. Is repentance a divine work or a human work?

An interesting example of repentance is found in Acts. Notice first, Peter does command repentance: 'Peter replied, "Repent and be baptised, every one of you, in the name of Jesus Christ for the forgiveness of your sins. And you will receive the gift of the Holy Spirit" (Acts 2:38).

Peter instructs people to repent. He expects them to be able to obey his order. What sort of people are they? They are people in whose hearts God has already been doing the thing we are talking about. As they had been listening to

233

Peter's sermon, their dismay had become intolerable. Notice the verse before the one I quoted: 'When the people heard this, they were cut to the heart and said to Peter and the other apostles, "Brothers, what shall we do?"' (Acts 2:37).

In matters of human volition it becomes difficult to untangle where God's action stops and ours begins. The closest explanation is to say that we can do nothing apart from God's gracious initiative. The human part is to respond to God's move. You're puzzled?

'Yes', you say. 'I wouldn't mind the kind of repentance you talk about, but supposing the Holy Spirit doesn't choose to give it to me. Supposing I never get this illumination. Right now I don't feel anything approaching what you have talked about.'

Then, I reply, you must ask for it. You must also acknowledge to God your need of it. He gave you the awareness of that need and you may count on God's faithfulness to give it to you in his time and way. He may or may not do so immediately, but he will not refuse what you ask. In the meantime you can do some heart-searching, asking him to quicken your heart as you do so.

Repentance and the gospel

The absence of the note of repentance from our gospel preaching may account for a low quality of Christian life among us. We certainly preach faith, but we forget that saving faith must be heart faith, not mere head faith. Paul tells us that 'if you confess with your mouth, "Jesus is Lord," and believe *in your heart* that God raised him from the dead, you will be saved. For it is *with your heart that*

234

you believe and are justified, and it is with your mouth that you confess and are saved' (Rom. 10:9–10, my italics). We talk about believing in our hearts, but fail to appreciate the profound difference between heart belief and 'believism'.

Our tendency to be obsessed with numbers of converts contributes to this. We are statistics crazy. In focusing on results and their import-ance, we may, without being aware of what we are doing, look for compliance in verbal responses rather than sensing what the Holy Spirit may be doing in the person we counsel. We produce what I have elsewhere referred to as 'butterflies that can't fly', in a fuller discussion of repentance.[6]

Moths and butterflies emerge from cocoons where they have concealed their chrysalis forms. To watch their struggle to free themselves is to watch the drama of life struggling to escape death. Strands of a glutinous substance hinder their emergence, attached as they are to their cocoon-tomb. The battle to free their wings from similar strands looks particularly painful. You can cut the strands to help them, but what you will wind up with is a partially formed butterfly that can't fly. It needs to struggle or it will never attain its full development, the full spread of its wings. The absence of evidence of life and power in the lives of many Christians has a similar cause.

How a great Welsh revival began

What happens then to Christians who can't 'fly'? Are they stuck with their spiritual disability, con-demned to spiritual wheelchairs, eternally mem-bers of the spiritually handicapped? By no means. Repentance is not only for the unsaved, as I wrote earlier, but for Christians. In another book I quoted from the diary of a man who was present at the beginning of the nineteenth-century revival in Wales. The congregation of a small Protestant church had assembled for the Wednesday business meeting, resentful about the previous Sunday's sermon and determined to express their resentment. Here is an extract from the diary:

> One of the elders got up and said it was a very difficult thing for a man to say 'Amen' under a ministry he felt condemning him; and as he said these things he sat down as if fainting away. At this moment, there was something (I cannot say what it was, but that it was *something* that neither I nor any one else had ever felt before) went through the whole congregation, until every one put down his head and wept! The following week the two churches, Wesleyan and Calvinistic Methodists, united to keep prayer meetings every night.[7]

They wept over their sins, like the men and women in the meeting on the east coast of Canada. However, it is not their weeping that is important here – we have already discussed the issue of the emotions of repentance. The importance of what took place lies in the fact that when God brings Christians to repentance, revivals can begin. In nineteenth-century Wales a revival followed, sweeping the country, changing the nation's values and behaviour. We need more Christians who weep for the same reasons the Welsh Christians wept in their little chapel.

Repentance is on-going. It is the norm of daily Christian living. We may not weep every day; weeping is only secondary to seeing certain issues clearly. Nevertheless Christians are those who have a sustained attitude of repentance. C. S. Lewis maintains that

> The repentance God desires of us is not just contrition over particular sins; it is also a daily attitude, a perspective.
>
> Repentance is the process by which we see ourselves, day by day, as we really are: sinful, needy, dependent people. It is the process by which we see God as he is: awesome, majestic and holy. ... And [it] so radically alters our perspective that we begin to see the world through God's eyes, not our own. Repentance is the ultimate surrender of the self.[8]

Such an attitude is not learned in a day. It involves a process of learning, an on-going Christian discipleship. Lewis comments on this discipline: 'It is something much harder than merely eating humble pie. It means unlearning all the self-conceit and self-will that we have been training ourselves into for thousands of years. It means killing part of yourself, undergoing a kind of death.'[9]

Changed behaviour

I have already made it clear that the test of true repentance is permanent behavioural change. There is no such thing as instantaneous sanctification, but in repentance major obstacles to on-going sanctification are removed. There are also particular results that are very interesting.

For instance, confession of sin has a limited, but very real, place in Christian experience, but when it should occur, profound shame can hold it back. One sign of true repentance is that the fear and shame of exposure are for ever removed. I believe that Finney was profoundly mistaken when he stated that revival can actually be brought about by our 'breaking up fallow ground in our hearts', however valuable that exercise may be.

Charles Finney did know, however, the difference between true and false repentance. He describes the phenomenon: 'He who has only false repentance resorts to excuses and lying to cover his sins, and is ashamed of his repentance. ... Instead of that ... openhearted ... frankness, you see a palavering, smooth-tongued, half-hearted mincing out of something that is intended to answer the purpose of a confession, and yet to confess nothing.'[10]

A California scientist I knew lost all his fear of people's finding out about his seduction of a younger man. He longed to face the church members where the incident had occurred, to express his pain and to ask for pardon. The discovery of his own ability to look people in the eye was a revelation to him. Repentance brings about a profound awareness of our forgiveness and our acceptance before God. It is revealed to our hearts in a manner that differs profoundly from mere intellectual understanding.

It was a revelation to a young woman whom God touched in the meeting I described earlier.

Two mornings later she told my wife, Lorrie, and me, 'I can walk through the precinct now and smile at people. I'm not ashamed any more. I can look right at people, right into their eyes!'

Righting wrongs and hating sin

Then there is the matter of making amends for past wrongs, always a right principle, though one that in no way cancels the guilt of the original sin. Those who know true repentance truly *want* to make restitution where it is possible to do so. Not only do they know they should, but nothing will hold them back from doing so. Says Finney, emphasizing this aspect of repentance: 'The thief has not repented while he keeps the money he stole.'[11]

Most of us acknowledge sin is bad. We know we should not sin and that sin displeases God. Yet few of us know a burning hatred of the thing itself. Thomas Watson, the Puritan, tells us that this fear and loathing of sin is yet another result of a true work of repentance in our hearts: 'A true penitent is a sin-loather. If a man loathe that which makes his stomach sick, much more will he loathe that which makes his conscience sick.'[12]

The sins we most need to loathe here in the West are sins like covetousness, greed, unwillingness to forsake all *in our hearts* that we might follow Jesus. I have insisted all along in this book that it is the heart attitude that matters, not whether we are in fact rich or poor. You can be poor and greedy, or rich and free from greed and the need to cling to your riches. Riches are powerfully seductive and difficult to be immune to. They bring the influence and even the power of mammon into our homes. But it is not a sin to possess them, only to be ruled by them. It is the *love* of money that is wrong, for I find myself serving whatever god I love. On the other hand I may give away all I have, yet, gripped by an illicit love, grow envious of those who have more, and judge them.

Is your heart free from mammon's lust? If not, it will be futile to pray that the church repent of lust until God has given you repentance about your own lust. Firm decisions apart from repentance may or may not enable you to quit a particular sin, but they will not stop you from lusting. However, if and when God grants you repentance, you will hate and loathe the lust of money and things, fleeing from it in disgust and terror. And the deeper the repentance, the greater the loathing, the terror, the disgust.

When the Son makes you free – you get to be free.

The future of the church

Our need for personal repentance, however, must never prevent us from praying about the future of the church. And about that future there are basically only two views. One view is that God will provide an escape hatch for the church (perhaps in the form of a secret rapture) at the point where she is about to be overwhelmed by evil's growing triumphs in the world. The other (the old Puritan and Reformed view) that before Christ returns the gospel will triumph spectacularly throughout the earth, with whole nations turning to God through the witness of a converted Israel and a gloriously triumphant church.[13]

Evil will flourish. Of this there is no doubt. The

night will grow darker. If we are appalled in any way about what is happening around us, we have only begun to see the unleashed furies of the blackness. The final Dark Ages are beginning. Humankind will dwell for many days without sun to light its gloom or shelter from the furies of the storm. And the church, like Hosea's bride, will suffer with it.

Yet there is no need to become feverishly addicted to those publications featuring experts on the prophetic Scriptures, in a needless panic to understand the details of the divine timetable. During the Second World War, when bombs rained ruin from the skies on Britain, some self-styled experts argued fiercely about the precise manner in which the war would end, tirelessly debating the fate of the Italians, the role of the Americans in France, scheduling and rescheduling the order of events. These 'experts' argued inside bomb shelters while London burned.

Other people wore helmets to protect their heads from the hot, jagged shrapnel that fell like lethal hailstones, dug among the rubble of ruined homes and factories, dragged men and women from burning ruins, drove ambulances. Yet others looked through gun sights around the city or flew tiny fighter planes beneath the stars, also peering through gun sights.

Some talked. Some fought. Doubtless the experts felt in some obscure way that the war was in their hands. Psychologically they needed to feel in control, and their talk, their pseudo-expertise, gave them the security that bomb shelters alone could not provide. Meanwhile, the real war was going on where shrapnel fell and bombs exploded.

It is so today. We are called to fight, not to be experts on the end times. We are called to bear witness in life or death to the King of Glory. That is why I tend to espouse the Puritan view of the church's future, rather than the views that began to be popularized during the nineteenth century. I prefer Church Triumphant to Church-Rescued-through-Escape-Hatch, even though I know my personal preferences will not determine the course of history.

I know that the view that is more likely to inspire our hearts with evangelistic fervour is the one more likely to be true, and the one to be preferred. Iain Murray maintains that the old view does this better. We boast about the modern missionary movement, and certainly we do well to give God thanks for all he has done through it. But Murray asserts that it has all along been hampered by the unfortunate eschatology of many of its members. He believes this had a detrimental effect on world evangelism.

> Millenarian missionaries have a style of their own. Their theory affects their work in the way of making them seek exclusively, or chiefly, the conversion of individual souls. The true and efficient missionary method is to aim directly, indeed, at soul winning, but at the same time to plant Christian institutions in heathen lands, which will, in time, develop according to the genius of the nationalities. . . .

Perhaps of all the tendencies of the new teaching none was worse than the effect it had on belittling the importance of the visible Church. In the minds of the generations of evangelicals who lived before the eclipse of the hope, the conversion of the nations was related to the Church of history.[14]

I would be a fool to end this book on a note of controversy. Indeed, I have no interest in adding to the endless, often self-righteous wrangles over end times. What really concerns me is the matter of whether we retire into the shelters to argue the course of the war or fight in the darkness to resist evil and rescue the perishing. Not that millenarians have been any less fervent in the battle than anyone else. It is just that at this point I sense that *talk* of the hope of Christ's imminent return is just that – talk. Gone are the days when people refrained from taking university training or from building another house simply because Christ's coming was 'just around the corner'.[15]

That sort of thinking still prevailed, even more than a hundred years after the origins of millenarianism, when I was still a child. We did not say with James, 'We will do thus and so if the Lord *will*', but 'if the Lord *tarry*'. Even then, we felt a little nervous about embarking on something when the Lord's coming was so close. We misunderstood the nature of that imminence. The end of the world was imminent then. It is still imminent. But it is more likely to happen now than it has ever been, and with it Christ's glorious coming.

Slowly, millenarians have come to behave as though they had the same hope as non-millenarians. Indeed many of us, millenarians and non-millenarians alike, seem to have settled down for the duration of our lives. We lack a vivid and compelling hope, the glory of the hope that quickened the hearts and behaviour of our Puritan forebears. They were certain that *the gospel would triumph throughout the whole earth, particularly in Muslim lands*. They belonged to the Church Triumphant. Call it triumphalism if you will – it was a blessed triumphalism. And unless hope of this sort prevails, all our enthusiasm will wane the more darkness supervenes.

I do not fear the darkness of the judgment that is coming, for I have been given a blessed hope and a blessed task. You say, 'Ah yes! The blessed hope of the soon return of the Lord Jesus!' True. But it is not to that hope I refer, but to the hope of what God will yet do in anticipation of his return.

My hope is the hope of Israel and the hope of the Gentiles. My hope is for repentance of the whole church. My hope (how my pulse races as I think of it!) is the hope that Israel will turn in repentance as a nation to their Messiah. My hope is that with that turning will come an outpouring of the Holy Ghost the like of which the earth has never seen – whole nations turning to God.

'Again I ask: Did [Israel] stumble so as to fall beyond recovery? Not at all! Rather, because of their transgression, salvation has come to the Gentiles to make Israel envious. But if their transgression means riches for the world, and their loss means

244

riches for the Gentiles, how much greater riches will their fulness bring!' (Rom. 11:11–12).

Paul is telling us that the salvation of Israel will mean that what we have experienced to date of the gospel's and the church's triumph will seem like the dimness of dawn in the light of the full day that now approaches. Let judgment come! Awful as it may be, a remnant will be saved – a vast remnant. The repentant will fill the earth. It is this hope that causes me to throw myself at the feet of the Saviour and with joy cry, 'Take my ageing body and my waning years and use me in some way to prepare for the return of the King!'

This hope is not mine alone. It is the classic hope that has sustained all who have struggled to maintain a gospel witness down the ages. Iain Murray gives us plenty of quotes on its nature from my Puritan and Reformed forebears. From Calvin:

> Whatever resistance we see today offered by almost all the world to the progress of the truth, we must not doubt that our Lord will come at last to break through all the undertakings of men and make a passage for his word. Let us hope boldly, then, more than we can understand; he will surpass our opinion and our hope.[16]

And from J. A. W. Neander, quoting from earlier periods in history: 'Strong and certain was the conviction of the Christians that the church would come forth triumphant out of its conflicts, and as it was its destination to be a world-transforming principle, would attain dominion of the world.'[17]

Neander is not talking about world dominion in the sense that reconstructionists think of it, but of the dominion over people's hearts and spirits by the Holy Spirit, and by truth.

Great as have been the triumphs of the gospel to date, the incalculable price Jesus paid at Calvary will bring a far, far greater in-gathering of souls before the end comes, even though it come soon.

That is why I must repeat: *In mercy, Lord, let judgment fall!* Terrible as it must be, what has to be will be. But grant us repentance also! Let an awakened Israel and a repentant and revived church go forth to win the nations!

A rider on a white horse is about to descend on the earth, a rider whose names are Faithful and True. He wears many crowns to remind us that he asserts his sovereignty, the sovereignty he always had and that he won back as man on our behalf. He is absolute ruler over this earth, ruler over every square inch of it. His robes are dipped in the blood of the coming judgments. Humankind is not his real enemy, so much as the dark lords who hold humankind in slavery. When he slays he will use the sword of his mouth, the Word of God. He is about to tread the winepress of the fury of God's rage. He is the King of kings and the Lord of lords (Rev. 19:11–21).

I will not live to see the full extent of it. But my heart burns to take part in its initiation. So I pray. I pray alone, and I pray with others. I am part of a chorus of prayer that gathers volume in all parts of the globe. Perhaps you are part of that same chorus. I pray about the coming judgments, and I plead for the pouring of repentance and revival on the church.

And already I hear the distant sound of a trumpet. The floodgates of heaven are beginning to swing open.

Notes

Chapter 1: The root of evil
1 Philip Yancey, 'How We Became the "Great Satan"', *Christianity Today*, 29 April 1991, p. 64.

Chapter 3: Paying the pastor
1 *Bound for Life* (Leicester: Inter-Varsity Press, 1990).

Chapter 6: Selling the sacred
1 C. S. Lewis, *The Abolition of Man* (New York: Macmillan, 1978), p. 25.
2 Plato, *The Republic*, 402.A.
3 Augustine, *The City of God*, XV.22.
4 Kenneth Grahame, *The Wind in the Willows* (London: Magnet, 1978 edition), pp. 134–136.
5 Josephus, *Antiquities of the Jews*, XX.vi.3.
6 Josephus, *Wars of the Jews*, VI.ii.4.

Chapter 8: The prophet's whip of cords
1 R. Alan Cole, *The Gospel According to St Mark*
   (Leicester: Inter-Varsity Press, 2nd edn. 1989),
   pp. 251–253.

Chapter 11: Treasure and heart
1 Dick France, 'Serving God or Mammon', *Third
   Way*, 18 May 1978.
2 F. C. Grant, *The Economy Background to the Gospel*; quoted in France, 'Serving God'.
3 France, 'Serving God'.
4 *Ibid*.

Chapter 13: The lashes of judgment
1 Oscar Cullmann explains the paradox of
   Satan's defeat and his continued rule on earth
   in his book *Christ and Time* (London: SCM,
   1951), p. 64. He compares the period since the
   resurrection with the period in the Second
   World War following the Allies' successful
   landing on the Normandy beaches. Once Allied
   forces were present in strength, victory was
   theirs. Yet the months that followed were the
   bitterest of the war, with appalling casualties.
2 Naturalism is what James Sire calls a *worldview*.
   It is the view of the universe commonly associated with the scientific enterprise – a universe
   that is self-existent and devoid of God. In his
   book *The Universe Next Door* (Leicester: Inter-
   Varsity Press, 2nd edn. 1988), Sire discusses the
   rise of naturalism and the philosophical and
   religious roots of its basic tenets.
3 'How Common is Pastoral Indiscretion?' *Leadership* 9 (Winter 1988), p. 12.
4 Francis Frangipane, *The Three Battlegrounds*

(Marion, Iowa: Frangipane, 1989), p. 100.

Chapter 14: God's plea for his people

1 A. W. Tozer, *The Pursuit of God* (Harrisburg, Pa.: Christian Publications, 1948), pp. 21–22.

Chapter 15: The glory of repentance

1 C. S. Lewis, *Mere Christianity* (New York: Collier/Macmillan, 1960), p. 109.

2 One of the best modern examples of this sort of weeping occurred in Chuck Colson when the Holy Spirit revealed his pride to him, some time before his conversion. See Charles W. Colson, *Born Again* (Old Tappan, NJ: Revell, 1976), pp. 116–117.

3 Jean LaFrance, *Pray to Your Father in Secret* (Sherbrooke, Quebec: Editions Paulines, 1987), p. 45.

4 *Ibid.*, p. 49.

5 Norman Grubb, *Rees Howells, Intercessor* (Fort Washington, Pa.: Christian Literature Crusade, 1984), pp. 29–30.

6 John White, *Changing on the Inside* (Guildford: Eagle, 1991).

7 *Ibid.*, pp. 8–9.

8 C. S. Lewis, *Mere Christianity*, p. 59. Also quoted in Charles Colson, *Against the Night* (Ann Arbor, Mich.: Servant), p. 140.

9 Lewis, *Mere Christianity*, p. 59.

10 Charles G. Finney, *True and False Repentance* (Grand Rapids, Mich.: Kregel, 1975), p. 19.

11 *Ibid.*, p. 17.

12 Thomas Watson, *The Doctrine of Repentance* (1668; Edinburgh: Banner of Truth, 1987, p. 45.

13 For a full exposition of this theme as the Puritans conceived it, see Iain Murray, *The Puritan Hope* (Edinburgh: Banner of Truth, 1971).

14 *Ibid.*, p. 205.

15 Contemporary Christians, whether millenarian or not, have little understanding of the powerful effect of the origins of the theories on contemporary Christianity, whether the origins are seen as those of the Irvingite movement or of J. N. Darby. Murray quotes F. W. Newman, speaking of his misunderstanding of immanence following his renunciation of the early millenarian views: 'The importance of this is, that it *totally forbids all working for earthly objects distant in time*. . . . For instance, if a youth had a natural aptitude for mathematics, and he asked, ought he to give himself to the study . . . my friend would have replied, that such a purpose would be very worldly if it were entertained by a worldly man. . . . Let the dead bury their dead. . . . Such studies cannot be eagerly followed by the Christian, except when he yields to unbelief.' Quoted in Murray, *Puritan Hope*, p. 203.

16 From Merle D'Aubigne, *History of the Reformation in Europe in the time of Calvin* (1876), 7:49, as quoted in Murray, *Puritan Hope*, p. xii.

17 Colson, *Against the Night*. This book draws a parallel between the barbarian invasion of Rome and the present: no civilization will last for ever, and we now face the West's time of darkness.

The Fight

JOHN WHITE

John White has written this book because he wants you to understand clearly what the Christian life is all about. He wants you to learn in the depths of your being that the eternal God loves you and plans only your highest good – more trust in him, more likeness to him.

But his love will bring pain as intense as your joy. For the Christian life is a fight....

"Reading *The Fight* is to inhale great draughts of fresh air into one's Christian life... This is the kind of book every 20th Century Christian should have on his book shelf."

Christian Weekly Newspapers

230 pages   Pocketbook

Inter-Varsity Press

The Masks of Melancholy

JOHN WHITE

Depression wears many masks. One sufferer just feels 'down'; another slashes his veins in lonely despair. Some whirl along in manic euphoria; others move with limbs of lead.

What is this monster that enslaves so many victims?
Is it spiritual? Physical? Demonic?
Why do Christians suffer too?
Why do people kill themselves?
How effective are today's therapies – counselling, drugs, ECT – and how do they work?

John White tackles these questions with the expertise of an experienced psychiatrist and the wisdom of a Christian steeped in God's Word. He offers guidance and encouragement to all who care for the depressed, whether as doctors, counsellors, pastors, friends or relatives.

"…this is a much needed book."   Today

"Distressed people need hope. This book is a means of encouraging that hope."   Renewal

252 pages   Pocketbook

Inter-Varsity Press

Parents in Pain

JOHN WHITE

Are you a parent?
How will you react if your child gets involved in
drugs, crime, sleeping around, alcoholism?
Will you blame yourself? your child?
society?

Whether you are a parent, potential parent, or
friend, this book will help you. It describes what
you can do and what you can't. Recognising the
limits of your responsibility will save you from
needless anguish and self-blame. This is a book
to help you meet difficulties with courage and
confidence.

"..offers the kind of help no Christian parent can
afford to miss." Family (formerly Life of Faith)

"This is an important book..." Renewal

242 pages Pocketbook

Inter-Varsity Press

People in Prayer

JOHN WHITE

Ten portraits of people in prayer to God.

People pleading, praising, confessing, interceding. People being changed as they draw closer to God.

God – wanting communication with human beings. With you.

"Go after this book – get it and read it! It will challenge and disturb but you will not regret it."
Grace Magazine

"...the contents proved so helpful. At all times practical, open, and in touch with our own times."
Reaper (New Zealand)

"This is a wholesome book, penetrating in its insight and profound in its encouragements."
Life and Work

"It is impossible to read this book without being driven to the Master's feet, with one simple petition, "Lord, teach us to pray"."
Christian Herald

160 pages   Pocketbook

Inter-Varsity Press

We hope that you have enjoyed this book. You may like to use this form to order other titles in the **John White** collection:

The John White Collection

08555	_____	Bound for life............................ ....£3.50
0407X	_____	Eros defiled................................ ....£3.50
04827	_____	Excellence in leadership............ ....£3.25
03944	_____	Fight, The.................................. ....£3.95
09748	_____	Greater than riches.................... ....£8.95
0472X	_____	Healing the wounded (with K.Blue)...£3.95
04428	_____	Masks of melancholy, The........ ....£4.25
04142	_____	Parents in pain........................... ....£3.95
04010	_____	People in prayer......................... ....£3.50
04622	_____	Race, The.................................. ....£3.95
04940	_____	Shattered mirror, The................ ....£2.25

These titles, along with many other IVP books, are available from your local bookshop. In cases of difficulty please return this form to Mickleover Books, marking clearly the titles you would like to receive. Please include your payment, including the cost of postage and packing:

UK: £1.00....for one or two books   £2.00....for three or four books
     £2.50....for five or more books

N.B. This service is only available to UK Mainland customers.

Name:_____

Address:_____

_____

I enclose payment of: £_____   or,

Please debit my VISA/MASTERCARD No.:_____

Expiry date____/____/____.   Signed:_____

Send this form to: Mickleover Books, 16 Hobart Close, Mickleover,
                   Derby DE3 5LJ

We reserve the right to change the price of these books and to increase postal rates in accordance with our carrier.